# KEVIN SMITH

# KEVIN SMITH

## HIS FILMS AND FANS

COMPILED AND EDITED BY

DAVID GATI

SCHIFFER
PUBLISHING

4880 Lower Valley Road · Atglen, PA 19310

# CONTENTS

## *CLERKS* [1994]: CONSUMERISM                                         14

In a world that felt commercialized, Kevin thought we were becoming part of consumer culture. From early on, before Kevin was a brand, nobody had really tapped into this idea of work that was repetitive, unskilled, low-level, and low-paying. The fans saw themselves reflected in this film, stuck in similar dead-end retail jobs.

## *MALLRATS* [1995]: REBELLION                                        42

Kevin initially struggled with connecting to a larger audience. It was a challenge for him, with his independent spirit to make a Hollywood formula film. He portrayed rebellious youth in the film, and it was his rebel fans who would ultimately support him.

## *CHASING AMY* [1997]: BUILDING THE RELATIONSHIP                      52

By sharing his private life, Kevin showed how we're all looking for more than just a casual relationship. Kevin meets Joey Lauren Adams and decides that being honest means putting his relationship in the film. The fans glommed on to the fact that he revealed his comic-loving, emotionally-stunted self on-screen.

# INTRODUCTION

**I BECAME A FAN OF KEVIN SMITH** after listening to his podcasts in 2011, which was around the time he started going full force into podcasting. Over many years, I followed the stories he told of the films he was making (*Red State*, *Tusk*, *Yoga Hosers*) or sometimes his earlier films. It was this sharing of his life, the way he would recollect or bullshit through his various podcasts (*SModcast*, *Jay & Silent Bob Get Old*, *Hollywood Babble-On*, *Red State of the Union*, *Film School Fridays*, *SMovieMakers*, *Plus One*, *Fat Man on Batman*), that opened up the idea of how much there was to know about him. And it was this avalanche of content, which could be overwhelming, that eventually led me back to his films.

After five years of listening to him, I started collecting these stories and putting them together, going through hundreds of hours of podcasts, Q&As, interviews, and behind-the-scenes documentaries. I found on-set stills and candid photos that complemented his filmography. Yet, I still didn't know if I really knew Kevin Smith. I was still missing something from the story of Kevin's filmmaking journey. Then I thought that his fans could help me better see him through their art or writing. That was when I finally began to understand him. Ultimately, this is a story told by Kevin as well as by his fans.

Kevin Smith began his filmmaking career as a fan. His connection to fans comes from his own creative spark, born as a fan. His films reference pop culture and are devoted to his own self-contained universe. That's probably why he's sustained a career for almost thirty years. Like the films themselves, we see the influences in Kevin's work. *Clerks* is an ode to Frank Capra's common man. *Mallrats* is a love letter to John Hughes and teen-titty comedies of the '80s. *Chasing Amy* is a comic-book geek's fantasy grounded in reality. *Dogma* is a filthy adaptation of the Bible. *Jay and Silent Bob Strike Back* is self-referential, parodying his own characters. *Jersey Girl* is similar to more serious work, like *Ordinary People* and *Kramer vs. Kramer*. *Clerks II* is his take on a sequel. *Zack and Miri Make a Porno* is a riff on porn and romantic comedies. *Cop Out* is his version of an action comedy. *Red State* is an homage to Tarantino. *Tusk* is his spin on horror. *Yoga Hosers* is where *Clueless* meets *Gremlins*. *Jay and Silent Bob Reboot* is a return to the beginning. And *Clerks III*, just like *The Wizard of Oz*, is his way home.

Within this context, we can reflect on his films through the stories he's told to his fans as well as photos, fan art, and social media posts. As Kevin continues making films, we'll follow his journey because he brings us along for the ride.

# A BRIEF VISUAL HISTORY OF KEVIN

"This is me, my sister Virginia, and my brother Donald in a
pair of family portraits taken in 1970 and 1985."
—Kevin Smith

Henry Hudson High School friends Ernie
O'Donnell, Mike Bellicose, and Kevin, 1986

"This photo [of dad Donald Smith] was taken at
the party after Harley's baptism."
—Kevin Smith, 1999

Kevin and his mom in front of the hospital where he was born. He posted this photo on Instagram for his 47th birthday.

Kevin with his wife Jen and daughter Harley

**thatkevinsmith** Behind me and Mom is Riverview Hospital in #redbank, #newjersey. We were both here 47 years ago, when I sprang forth from her nether regions on 8/2/1970. After a whirlwind trip to #londonfilmandcomiccon and #notredamecathedral In #paris, it felt fitting that our mother-son journey abroad end where it truly began: here at #riverview. Thank you to everyone for all the birthday well-wishes you've sent me today. And thanks for supporting me & my bullshit for nearly 25 years; it makes every day feel like it's my birthday. #KevinSmith #birthday #leo #mom #amazinggrace #nj

Kevin signing for fans in Westwood Village, near UCLA, 2006. *Photo by K.C. Alfred / SDU-T / ZUMA Press, Inc. / Alamy Stock Photo*

Kevin fanning out with Deborah Foreman at a screening of *Valley Girl*, 2011. *Courtesy of Film at Lincoln Center / Andrew Levengood*

**KEVIN SMITH**

# VIEW ASKEWNIVERSE

## AN OVERVIEW OF THE INTERCONNECTEDNESS OF KEVIN'S FILMS

VIOLETA960 | SANTIAGO, CHILE |
"VIEW ASKEW RELATIONSHIPS," 2008
"A CHART WITH ALL THE CANON RELATIONSHIPS IN THE VIEW ASKEWNIVERSE"

BLUE = FRIENDSHIP        SOLID = CURRENT
RED = ROMANTIC           D A S H E D = PAST
GREEN = FAMILY

# CLERKS

1994

# CONSUMERISM

**FROM THE BEGINNING,** Kevin Smith was a salesman. Working in convenience stores around Highlands, New Jersey, he always knew he could get a minimum-wage job. Selling crap at Quick Stop could have been his life. He found like-minded misfits who loved comics, hockey, rap, heavy metal, drugs, sex, and movies. And that might have been enough. But it wasn't. So Kevin decided to make a film about these people who serve us, and it all began as a clerk.

This film was never really expected to be released. It was shot in black and white and used unknown actors; when finished, no one who worked on it thought it would ever be seen again. But those two slackers behind the counter at Quick Stop were like their counterparts who worked in department stores, waited on tables in diners and cafés, bartended, and did a million other bad retail jobs. No one thought that it would be picked up by any studio, let alone the most prestigious film distributor of the '90s, Miramax. It turns out the fans mattered more than the studio. They loved the film because they related to Dante and Randal. Years later, a fan's campaign led to the movie being honored by the National Film Preservation Board as one of twenty-five inductees to their annual registry. In reference to this honor, Ethan Anderton wrote in */Film* on December 11, 2019, that *Clerks* represents "the spirit of independent cinema in young filmmakers."

# THE BEGINNING

**Kevin Smith** [*speaking to friend Vincent Pereira*]: I get the job at Quick Stop in 1989. I was looking through the want ads in the paper, in the *Asbury Park Press*, and there was an ad for a video-store clerk. And that was my dream job. "Oh my God, being able to work in a video store. To take movies home. To watch movies. To have access to new releases. I'm going in."

And so I go in and meet with Mr. Thapar, Tralochan Thapar. And he runs Quick Stop and RST. His family owns it. In fact, the initials RST stand for the names of his family. Rajiv, his son. Tralochan was his name. Sarala was his wife. That's RST Video. So I go in to meet with Mr. Thapar. The video store's locked, which is a leitmotif of that video store. Sign telling me to go to Quick Stop. I go over. I meet Mr. Thapar. He goes [*imitates Indian accent*], "Come, come. Come next door. We will talk." And he takes me to RST Video, sits me down behind the counter. I'll never forget. Remember those little dopey stools, tiny, like the ones you put your feet on? We were sitting on two of those stools, low to the floor, six inches from the floor, and he's looking at my resume that I filled out. And the thing he focused in on, he goes, "You have worked at convenience stores before."

And I had tons of convenience-store experience. I'd worked at Crowser's. I'd worked at Cohen's. I'd worked at Bayview Deli, the Galley Deli. Convenience stores were my bag. Easy job. So I said, "Yeah, yeah, yeah."

He's going, "We also own the convenience store next door. Would you be willing to work both at the video store and sometimes at the convenience store?"

I didn't want to work at the convenience store. I just wanted the video-store job. But I was like, "If this is going to help, fuck it." I was like, "I'll work Quick Stop, I guess. Whenever you want, but what I really want to do is work here." And I got the job.

Kevin in front of Quick Stop, 1994
*RGR Collection / Alamy Stock Photo*

# SLACKER

**Kevin Smith** [*speaking to friend Vincent Pereira*]: Whatever August 2, 1991, was. I think it's a Friday. But maybe it was a Saturday night. I can't remember now. But it's my birthday. We're sitting in the store, and I want to say it is Friday 'cause I was like, "Hey, man. We're closing up at 10:30. You want to go see a movie or something?" And there was nothing we wanted to go see at Hazlet. We'd seen everything, but we were talking about going to New York, go see this *Slacker* movie. And watching *Slacker*, that's the movie that changes things for me. That's the movie where I'm looking at it, going like, "This doesn't really seem that difficult."

**Vincent Pereira:** Now was it in the Hoberman review [in the *Village Voice*]—did they talk about it only costing thirty-something thousand dollars, that it was shot in Austin? 'Cause you knew all that before going in to see it.

**KS:** Definitely. It was part of anywhere they talked about *Slacker*, and again this wasn't the Internet where I went online. You couldn't. So the only place to read about it was going to be *Village Voice, New York Post, Daily News*, or *Filmmaker* magazine, one of the independents or something like that. There weren't many sources, not like now. So I did know it was a low-budget film. I think it's because of the "Reels and Deals" article, which I still have. It was a movie being talked about places, that you could figure out what the budget was because Richard Linklater was candid about it.

**VP:** For some reason, I thought that *Slacker* cost a little more than Clerks. I thought it was in the low thirties. I could be wrong.

**KS:** That was the thing. I always talk about, "The budget of *Clerks* was $27,575," but we never had a budget. That's just what *Clerks* cost. We never really said. We never wrote down what shit should cost or had a budget, per se. The *Slacker* number was incredibly low. I knew that. It was under $50,000 and that was within striking distance. When you hear about the making of *Stranger Than Paradise*, you're still talking about an independent film that was made for $120,000 in the mid-'80s; $120,000 is still a $500,000 to $750,000 movie today, so you couldn't just come by that kind of money.

So we see *Slacker*, like I said. It's a transforming experience because it all seemed possible now. And Richard Linklater mixes up all sorts of formats. He's got 16mm; he's got Super 8; he's got a Pixelvision camera. Remember he used the Fisher-Price Pixelvision. The party scene. It's just a celebration of indie film, man. He was indie film. Like, "Look at me! Look at all I can do, man. This is the edge and I'm on it, bitch!" Come out of that movie, man, I'd never thought about being a filmmaker. I'd thought about writing for Vincent and helping him make movies and shit, but never thought about doing it myself, about directing. Suddenly, *Slacker* makes me go, "Well, I don't know. If that counts, I think I could direct as well. I think maybe I can say 'Action!' And fuckin' I know how shit should sound. I went to that acting class. And I remember telling people what to do and shit. I just innately knew how shit should sound, so maybe, maybe . . ." I'm thinking about all this as I'm watching the movie. We leave and we get in the car and we're driving home and we get to outside the Holland Tunnel. Tell me if I'm wrong. It's just as we're getting to the toll plaza. I had to say it out loud. And Vincent's the first person I ever said it out loud to. And I said, "I think I want to be a filmmaker."

# FILM SCHOOL

**Kevin Smith:** I start looking at going to film school, but I feel old 'cause I'm twenty-one at this point. Once again, the *Village Voice* provides everything. And there's an ad every week. We see it in the *Village Voice*.

**Vincent Pereira:** For the Vancouver Film School.

**KS:** I had already went to film school. Did it every night right there at Quick Stop behind the counter. Or at RST. Or all those many rides up into the city to see independent flicks.

**VP:** Quentin says the same thing too. He considers the video store his film school.

**KS:** There was an article that John Brodie had written in *Variety*, circa 1994. It was a really good think piece. He called it "The Video Store Generation." He was like, "You, Quentin Tarantino, Roger Avary. You're these auteurs that are coming out of these video stores. Your film schools are watching movies in the video store." It was pretty cool 'cause there weren't many more in that class or in that subgenre of filmmakers who worked at video stores. And it became kind of a cliché after a certain point. Kids working in a video store wanted to make movies. But [Tarantino] was the same kind of way. Self-taught.

I don't want to do four years. And then I remembered that ad, and I'm like, "It says nine months." Call 'em up. "What's the deal?" They were like, "It's eight months, nine grand Canadian." So it was cheaper. But it was eight months in and out. And I was like, "Really? It's a degree program."

They're like, "No. You just get a certificate that says you completed a technical program." And I was like, "It's gotta be as good as a fuckin' film school degree. Can you send me the paperwork?"

They sent me the application. I filled it out. You had to write an essay on why you were a filmmaker and then send it in with a check. And lo and behold, a couple of weeks later, I got this acceptance letter. And I remember being like, "Holy shit, man! They must see the fuckin' talent from my essay. They must feel the power. They must know I'm a filmmaker."

I got there and they were like, "You're in class 25." I was like, "What does that mean?" They were like, "This is the twenty-fifth time we've done this. And we have twenty per class." So I was like, "Are there twenty people in this class?" "Oh yeah. There's twenty for the next few classes."

It was clear that the eight months I was looking for was not the eight months that they were giving. I just wanted to go in and learn how to use shit. So I remember going to the office and just asking the question. I was like, "Hey, man. If I dropped out, do I get my money back?"

And they were like, "Well, we give you a percentage of your tuition, but only if you drop out by month four. If you drop out one day after the four-month mark, we keep the rest."

So, suddenly there was a ticking clock. Suddenly I was like, "Shit, man. I got a few weeks to make a decision here."

Bryan [Johnson] had been a decent role model. He had went away to guitar school once in California, and he dropped out. So I was like, "If dropping out is good enough for Big Bry, [and] there's no better upstanding individual than Bryan Johnson, it's good enough for me." So I weighed a certainty against a doubt. And the certainty was, "If I leave now, I'm going to walk away with 4,500 bucks. I could take that money and put it into a production." And the doubt that I had was, "I doubt I'll ever finish. I doubt I'll ever continue on this path." But the certainty I knew was, I had the money.

# FIRST VERSION OF THE SCRIPT

**Vincent Pereira:** You had a one-page treatment—well, not really a treatment. It was a one-page synopsis of *In Convenience* [the original title] and it read like a David Lynch film. The midnight to 6:00 a.m. shift.

**Kevin Smith:** And these monsters, human monsters would come in.

**VP:** Weird people, and the guy thinks he's going crazy. And then I started reading pages and I'm like, "What the hell is this? This is funny . . ."

**KS:** It's true. I'd worked at convenience stores for a while. I worked the midnight shift at Crowser's at one point, in Atlantic Highlands. So I'd come up with this story, a version of *Clerks*. I was always attracted to the convenience store. Social meeting place. They're everywhere. It's in every fuckin' community. Nobody had really put a spotlight on it. So I decide to get the fuck out of [Vancouver Film School]. I'm like, "You know what? I'll fuckin' come home. Put my money into *Clerks*." But I didn't know what *Clerks* would be. There was this version of *Clerks* where it could have been this Lynchian, almost kind of like— what was that movie we fuckin' loved? *Jacob's Ladder*. Humans, but there's a hint of a fuckin' demon tail. Something's off or whatever. And the dude on shift is like, "Am I slowly going crazy?" I remember there was shit like some dude sitting there eating a hand. And the clerk is trying not to say anything about it as the dude calmly sits there and has this conversation about the weather or sports while he's eating a human hand. You know, maybe trying a little too hard.

I come back from Vancouver. I did have the first scene written by that point, though. The first scene I ever wrote was "I don't appreciate your ruse, ma'am." Vincent knew I was coming back. I had to go to Quick Stop to be like, "Hey, man, I want to shoot a movie here."

And Mrs. Thapar was like [*imitates female Indian accent*], "Great. Can you come back to work now?" And I was like, "Uh . . . yeah. Really?" She's like, "Bryan and his girlfriend are driving us crazy. He is driving this store out of business, I tell you, with the free soda." I was like, "I'll come back and work here only if you let me shoot a movie." They were like, "What?"

"I want to make a film here. I went to film school, so I want to make a movie here." They were like, "Oh yes, of course. Do whatever you want, but come back to work." So I went back to work and I started writing *Clerks*.

I had remembered seeing an interview with Robert Rodriguez or hearing an interview he did. I think it was on the *Howard Stern Show*, and he was like, "Look, I just took stock of everything I had. A lot of people write movies, write about things they have no access to, write about situations they'll never be able to shoot." He's going, "I just started with like, 'What do I have?'" He's like, "I have a guitar case. I've got a turtle. I've got a bus. I'll write these things into the movie."

So, I don't know, it just made sense to me. It's like, "Wow. Well, what do I have? What's handy here?" I was like, "What can I write about?" Then I was like, "Wait a second, man. I've never seen a convenience-store movie." There'd been no TV show about it or anything, and it was just like, "I don't know, maybe this is it. Maybe I shouldn't look any further than fuckin' right around me. This is a movie set, isn't it?" So I start writing *Clerks* and I start feeding Vincent pages. And it isn't the fuckin' Lynchian weirdness. It's more like a portrait of our fuckin' lives.

# MEET JEFF ANDERSON

**Kevin Smith:** I'd gone to high school with Jeff . . .

**Vincent Pereira:** And he was a frequent customer.

**KS:** He was coming into RST because he lived on Grand Avenue in Atlantic Highlands. So if you're living in Atlantic Highlands, particularly where he lived, you would go to the Video Movie House, which was over in the Foodtown parking lot. But Video Movie House was the most popular video store, so all the new releases were always gone. They had a thriving fuckin' business at that point. So he had discovered RST. One day, while I wasn't working, he walked in and he saw, "Holy shit! Brand-new releases sitting in this shelf. Nobody knows about this hole-in-the-wall joint, man." And then one day he came back to return videos and get new shit, and he's like, "Smitty, you work here?"

And I was like, "Hey, man." Jeff and I went to high school together and we weren't super close in high school. We ran in different circles but certainly respected one another's work, if you will. And then after high school, we hung out for one summer where I hung out with him and Vic Guerra, and then that was about it. So hadn't seen each other in a couple years, and here he was coming into RST. We talked movies and shit like that. And then the old school talk, talked about Hudson and about people we went to school with.

Then one day he came in and I had the word processor, which was like an electric typewriter keyboard and then you plugged in this drive that had hard micro discs. Then it had this green-screen monitor that you hooked into the electric typewriter. I'm sitting there doing rewrites on *Clerks*, trying to bring it down in page length, and Jeff comes in and he's like, "What are you doing? What's this?" He thought it was a video game.

And I was like, "It's a word processor. I'm working on a script." He's like, "A script? Like, movie script?" I said, "Yeah, yeah. I think I want to try to make a movie. You know, I saw this movie, *Slacker*," and I tell him the story and stuff. And he's like, "Get outta here. That's fuckin' weird." And I was like, "Yeah, yeah."

So he periodically would be like, "What's going on with the movie?"

Then one day he came in, dropping off tapes, picking up new tapes and stuff. He's like, "What's going on with the movie these days?" I was like, "We're having our auditions tomorrow night." He's like, "Get outta here." I said, "Yeah, man. First Avenue Playhouse." And he's like, "I don't live far from there at all."

I said, "You should come by, man. Belli's [Michael Bellicose] coming. Ernie's [Ernie O'Donnell] gonna be there." I said, "Come on down, man. You should come, be in the flick." And he was like, "Maybe I will, maybe I will."

I didn't think he would, but he showed up. He popped by that night. He knew a lot of people there. Ernie, Bellicose, Betsy Broussard was there. So he didn't come prepared with anything. He'd never acted before in his life. None of the plays in high school or anything like that. He didn't bring a piece, like everybody else. If you've seen the *Clerks* Tenth Anniversary DVD, you see the auditions. Brian O'Halloran is doing a piece from *Wait Until Dark*. It's Dante doing *Psycho*. Marilyn did a piece where she cried. And we all went back to the Marina Diner, which is where Jay and Silent Bob meet Holden in *Chasing Amy*. And we were in that corner booth by the windows—me, Walter [Flanagan], Vincent—sitting there, going, "Can you believe that woman cried? It was just so weird. She just started crying. That's an amazing actress. We gotta put her in the movie." We liked Brian O'Halloran. And we had a Randal, but it wasn't the Randal. There was no choice. By this point, I had given up on the notion of doing it.

**VP:** That's right! You were going to do Randal.

**KS:** But I was like, "I can't memorize this and work at the store and direct the movie. And you know what? It should be somebody else." And we started looking for that person at the First Avenue Playhouse casting.

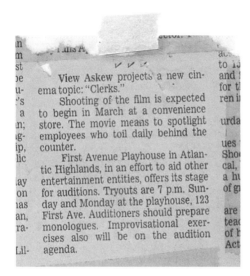

View Askew projects a new cinema topic: "Clerks."

Shooting of the film is expected to begin in March at a convenience store. The movie means to spotlight employees who toil daily behind the counter.

First Avenue Playhouse in Atlantic Highlands, in an effort to aid other entertainment entities, offers its stage for auditions. Tryouts are 7 p.m. Sunday and Monday at the playhouse, 123 First Ave. Auditioners should prepare monologues. Improvisational exercises also will be on the audition agenda.

"This is the *Clerks* audition notice we put in the *local* paper back in 1993. . . . The journey from script to screen began right here. Putting it in the newspaper made the dream of making a movie feel more real. And before we knew it, reality became a dream come true. Big changes start small. And this little bit of ink would transform my life."

—Kevin Smith

Brian O'Halloran as Dante and Jeff Anderson as Randal, 1994. *AF Archive / Miramax / Alamy Stock Photo*

# READING RANDAL

**Kevin Smith** [*speaking to actor Jeff Anderson*]: So I called you up and said, "Can I come over and read the script with you?" You were like, "Yeah, sure. Okay."

In retrospect, it's such a weird thing. We didn't hang out. If I called up [producer Scott] Mosier and said that, he would have been like, "Yeah, all right. Come over." But I was calling up a dude who I wasn't that tight with. And I was like, "Can I read my magic script with you?" It's just such a weird thing. Like, it probably sounded like I was trying to come on to you. I'd be there in the room and I'd be like, "Fuck the script. Kiss me."

And you're like, "Oh, God! He's doing it again." But you said, "Yeah. I guess, come over." And we sat in your living room. You were living at your parents' house in Atlantic Highlands at this point. Sat in the living room and I read Dante and you read Randal and we read the whole script from top to bottom.

At the end of it, you closed the script and I was just like, "I think you should do this. I think you should play Randal."

# FINDING THE TEAM

**Kevin Smith:** Scott Mosier was a producer on almost everything I did. We were going to hire John Thomas to shoot *Clerks*. He was the guy that shot *Metropolitan*. And I loved *Metropolitan*, Whit Stillman's film. So I said, "All right, man. If this guy shot *Metropolitan*, *Metropolitan* got a theatrical release, and I know the name of Whit Stillman and shit, let's go with him because he shot a movie that's already gotten picked up." I found him in the back of the *AIVF* magazine. It was a film-zine kinda thing. And he was 1,000 bucks a week, but he came with his own equipment. So I was arguing for that with Scott. I was like, "Let's get this guy. I mean, he's 1,000 bucks, but he comes with his own equipment, so we don't have to rent the equipment and stuff."

And Scott's argument was, "Wouldn't you rather surround yourself with people that don't know more than you?" He's going, "There is definitely something we'll benefit from by having people on set who've shot a movie, but we've never done this before. And this is our first time out of film school. You didn't even fuckin' finish. And this is all your money." He's like, "Do you really want to be on set with somebody who's going, 'I don't know this guy.' Maybe he's a great guy, but what if he's a guy that's like, 'You guys are idiots. You don't even know what you're doing.' Right now, we live in this world where we can do it. If we bring somebody in who's like, 'Oh, you guys aren't ready . . .'"

I think Scott's biggest fear was we'd hire somebody—John Thomas, say—as a DP [director of photography], he'd come to set and be like, "This is not how it was done on Metropolitan." And suddenly, all that vision, all that aspiration, all the fire, piss, and vinegar just goes right in the toilet because someone who's a pro said no. So I think he was right. He said, "Let's use Dave."

And I was like, "Dave Klein?" 'Cause we went to film school together with Dave Klein.

He goes, "Yeah. And Dave's a shooter and he was in our class, so it's not like he's gonna know any more than us. So let's all be on the same level playing field."

# HOW TO PAY FOR IT

**Scott Mosier:** I didn't know how to budget a movie. I didn't know if it was possible. Kevin had sent me the article from *Filmmaker* magazine that Peter Broderick had written about budgets.

**Vincent Pereira:** Being that *Slacker* had only cost about $35,000 to make, Kevin figured that he had enough credit that he could make a film on that level just by maxing out his credit cards.

**Grace Smith** [Kevin's mother]: He was selling some of his comic book collection, statuettes and everything. And he was just hoping from there that he would have enough money to start.

Kevin met Scott Mosier at Vancouver Film School, and they continued making films together.
*Courtesy of Dave Klein, ASC*

# FILM STOCK

**Kevin Smith:** I remember we had to get a bunch of film from Kodak, and they give a 15 percent student discount if you went to film school. So we ordered a bunch of black-and-white stock to roll through our Arri SR2 that we'd also rented. And the guy slaps our film up on the counter and he goes, "I just need a student ID."

And I was like, "Mos [Scott Mosier], where's your student ID?"

He's like, "Well, I think I left my school ID downstairs in my school bag."

And so, rather than be beaten, we went down to the New School for Social Research and looked through the catalogue. There were two courses. One was "Roasting Suckling Pig" and the other was "Understanding Your Homosexuality." So, of course we went for the "Understanding Your Homosexuality" course. Went back up to Kodak, slapped the ID down. The dude had to give us the film, looking at us like, "Fuck. Beaten by these two bastards."

Used by permission of Media Entertainment, Inc.

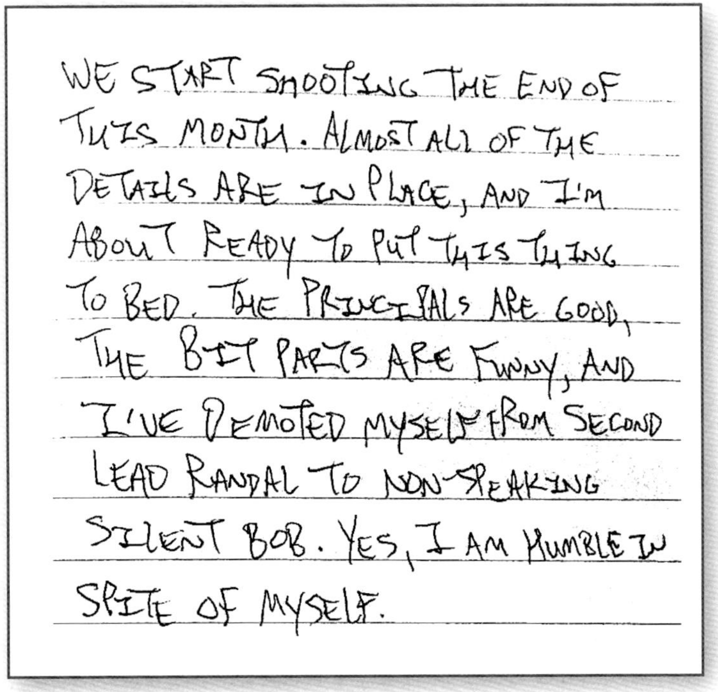

WE START SHOOTING THE END OF
THIS MONTH. ALMOST ALL OF THE
DETAILS ARE IN PLACE, AND I'M
ABOUT READY TO PUT THIS THING
TO BED. THE PRINCIPALS ARE GOOD,
THE BIT PARTS ARE FUNNY, AND
I'VE DEMOTED MYSELF FROM SECOND
LEAD RANDAL TO NON-SPEAKING
SILENT BOB. YES, I AM HUMBLE IN
SPITE OF MYSELF.

"From my *Clerks* pre-pro journal, an entry
dated 3/4/93 – less than 2 weeks before
we started shooting at Quick Stop."
–Kevin Smith

# SILENT BOB

**Kevin Smith:** There was the character of Silent Bob. I was intending to put a friend of mine from school, Mike Bellicose, in it. But I said, "Fuck Mike. I'm gonna do it, 'cause if this is the only movie we're ever going to make, I at least want to be in it so that years from now, when I'm still paying off my ridiculously large credit card bill, I can pop it in anytime I ever got a notion to direct another movie." I'd pop in the movie, see my greatest blunder, and be like, "Oh, yes. There's me. What an idiot." There were three dudes with barely any knowledge on cinema or how to put together a film or directing or producing or shooting. Complete fuckin' amateurs were able to pull together a movie that still holds up to this day. It was a real blessed accident. Three guys failing upwards every day for twenty-one days straight.

Used by permission of Media Entertainment, Inc.

José Malvárez | Portosín, Spain | "Daily Sketch 090:
Kevin Smith as Silent Bob," 2015

# PRODUCTION

**Scott Mosier:** Dave and I arrived there three or four weeks ahead of time. We had a plan. Kevin was working at the store, so that was the central office.

**David Klein** [cinematographer]: We scouted the Quick Stop. We looked at the other few locations we had. Actually, Ed Hapstak [gaffer] and I built a couple of fluorescents.

**Ed Hapstak:** I just chained some fluorescent lights up there, and I think we even put up some of my halogen work lights. Actually, we moved all the cigarettes. We took the cigarettes up from above the counter. The whole cigarette racks were gone, and we were basically bouncing light off of where the cigarettes would normally be.

**DK:** We got the camera from a place in New York, and it was an old Arriflex SR. Sounded like a fuckin' machine. Probably the loudest camera I've ever worked with. I think the look of that movie was mainly decided by the dollar. It was just more cost-effective to shoot black and white.

**SM:** This whole issue of color temperature . . .

**DK:** You've got fluorescents, but we've also got windows to deal with.

**SM:** If we shot in black and white, that was no longer something we'd even have to think about.

**DK:** And then we can use the tungsten lights that we have, mixed with the fluorescents that were there. Close the shutters. Kevin wrote that into the script—that someone jammed gum in the locks—and we don't have to worry about the windows and that's another color temperature.

*Clerks III* script, with original clapper, 2013

**KEVIN SMITH**

# WRAPPING UP

**Kevin Smith:** So we wrapped the movie. Wrapping was really walking from that store [Quick Stop] to . . .

**Scott Mosier:** Over here [RST Video]. We just had to return the equipment to New York. The Steenbeck [flatbed editor] came here. The Six-Plate [Movieola] came here to the video store.

First screening of *Clerks* at the Independent Feature Film Market Brian O'Halloran, Jeff Anderson, Marilyn Ghigliotti, Lisa Spoonauer, David Klein, Kevin, Scott Mosier, and Vincent Pereira, 1993

Marilyn Ghigliotti as Veronica Loughran, Kevin Smith as Silent Bob, Brian O'Halloran as Dante Hicks, Jeff Anderson as Randal Graves, and Lisa Spoonauer as Caitlin Bree, 1994 *Entertainment Pictures / Alamy Stock Photo*

# INDEPENDENT FEATURE FILM MARKET

**Kevin Smith:** October 3, 1993, was the IFFM [Independent Feature Film Market], the very first public screening of *Clerks*, which changed our lives. Although in that moment . . . No.

**Scott Mosier:** Well, it did. It created a reality.

**KS:** What was that? Explain . . .

**SM:** It created the momentary reality of failure.

**KS:** We entered *Clerks* in the IFFM long before Sundance. When we were making *Clerks*, that's all we were headed towards. That was the goal: to go to the IFFM. Submit it.

**SM:** And so you get a screening and then basically distributors, festival representatives, press, people come in and out of the screenings . . .

**KS:** I remember the whole cast and crew went. Brian O'Halloran, Lisa Spoonauer, Jeff Anderson, Marilyn Ghigliotti, me, Scott, Dave Klein, Vinnie Pereira, Ed Hapstak, Walter Flanagan. Ten [of us]. So, no Bryan Johnson, which is questionable and scandalous, but we weren't talking right then. And no Jason Mewes. A lot of people were like, "Where the fuck was Jay?" He didn't care one iota. He didn't remember we made a movie.

It's a Sunday morning. We weren't living in Red Bank or Highlands; we were living in Montclair, New Jersey. So it was like a half-hour ride. And remember, we'd gone three days that week. It was packed. You couldn't move down by Houston and Mercer, let alone once you get in the fuckin' Angelika, which is where it was held, the Angelika Film Center. All upstairs was packed. All downstairs was packed. We hoped Miramax would show up at our screening. Fuck, we hoped anybody would show up at our screening.

**SM:** But we expected a bunch of people. And then got there Sunday morning . . .

**KS:** Empty on the streets. Thin on the streets. So I was like, "Ah, they're all in the theater. Packed, lined, sitting, ready to go. They can't wait to see *Clerks*. They must have seen our handy handbill work earlier in the week."

I remember going into the theater and there was two people and one guy sitting up front and one lady off to the side. It was very fuckin' spartan. Like, hardly spartan. And that's the moment of failure Scott's talking about. I died. I know I died in that theater. This might all be a *Jacob's Ladder*–type existence, where every once in a while I see a tail coming out of Scott's pants, and shit like that. I'm like, "I don't get it. Am I dead or not? Are they going to zip up a bag?"

I know I died in that theater 'cause that was everything I was working toward. The dream. And we had almost accomplished the dream. We had a finished film. We were playing at the IFFM. But nobody was there to see it. I remember going through, as Stan Lee would say in *Mallrats*, "a rage of emotions." I was never one of those Tony Robbins "You-can-do-anything" [types], but it was survival. Otherwise, I would have fuckin' died in that theater. So I had to keep the level head of like, "All right. Yeah. This hurts. It hurts to fuckin' lose. And you miscalculated. Nobody's here and who gives a fuck? Black and white. Who are you, fuckin' Steven Spielberg? But you enjoyed it. And there's something worth watching up there."

And at the end of the screening, everyone who went was like, "Oh my God. That was awesome."

But I was like, "Yeah, that was awesome, but there was only fuckin' ten of us here, and those people and those people." But I remember being like, "Do it one more time before you say you'll never do this again, because you liked it."

And after the screening, there was nobody really to talk to. There was the one lady. She goes, "You made this?"

I said, "Yeah."

She goes, "You know people like this?"

I was surrounded by people like that and the cast. And I was like, "Yeah."

And she goes, "I got a theory that all the Nazis that ever died are reincarnated and populating New Jersey."

And I was like, "Ah. I never heard that theory." I don't even think I said something that clever.

**SM:** That was my life preserver. Thanks.

**KS:** I was about to die in there and I was glad I lived. Now I wish I had died a few minutes ago. And then she was like, "I guess I'll give you my headshot." She gave me her fuckin' headshot. She was an actress and she left.

There was another couple in the theater. And I never really talk about them. They gave me a thumbs-up. They were like, "That was really funny." But they didn't have any badge that said anything of any value whatsoever. So I was like, "Fuck your opinion. I'm ruined. Ruined! That means something if each of you pay $13,000 to watch it. Other than that, I'm fucked. Fucked!"

Scott was the one who talked to Bob Hawk. Bob Hawk had an ICI badge, Independent Consultation for Independents. I was not there for the conversation. What did he say? How did it go?

**SM:** My memory was [that] Bob really liked the movie, and I think he wanted to know, "Was there a tape in the library?" He was just asking me some questions. He was like, "Do you have any press?" That was it. He was like, "Do you have a press kit?" I was like, "Uh. Up by the thing." That's all I did.

**KS:** The "thing" was the mailbox. Everyone had their own mailboxes, so you could put a bunch of press kits in there. We stuffed mailboxes with press kits. Remember that? Making up like 50, 100 press kits. It was a folder with a sticker on it that said, "*Clerks*," with the screening date. And inside was a breakdown of the movie, description of the movie, the players; and then there was the press clipping, which the *Asbury Park Press* did, "Local Filmmakers Make Local Film." Scott and I, standing by the Steenbeck. And one of the other papers had something similar, so we could at least include it. So Scott directed Bob to the press kit.

# BOB HAWK / PETER BRODERICK / AMY TAUBIN

**Bob Hawk:** I was walking up the stairs. Peter Broderick was walking down the stairs. I said, "I just saw this movie. I think it's wonderful. It's called *Clerks*. I think you should see it."

**Peter Broderick:** Bob I'd known for a while, and I really took his recommendations seriously, so I made a point of getting the video cassette out of the library and going and sitting down and watching the film. And I thought it was absolutely great. And so the next day I was talking to Amy Taubin, who was a really good friend.

**Amy Taubin:** I was writing for the *Village Voice* and I had a column there. And I was covering the market. I had basically nothing to write about because there was nothing much of interest there.

**PB:** I said, "Amy, you gotta see *Clerks*."

**AT:** I got a number in Jersey.

**PB:** And I think she spoke to Kevin's mother. And Kevin's mother, if I remember, said, "You mean, somebody liked my son's movie?"

**Kevin Smith:** So we're all in this apartment and kind of dejected. And the phone rings. "Kevin, my name's Amy Taubin. I write for the *Village Voice*."

And I was like, "Yeah. I know who Amy Taubin is." I was like, "Who is this, man? Quit lying. Don't fuckin' yank my chain."

**AT:** I said, "No, no, no. This is Amy Taubin from the *Village Voice*, and I heard your film is great and I would like to see it."

**KS:** And I was like, "Is this really Amy Taubin?" I was like, "Do you know I have the article you wrote about Richard Linklater framed?"

She was like, "Well, this phone call just took a jump."

I was like, "Who told you this?"

She was like, "I'm not at liberty to say, but if you could send me a tape, I might be able to write about it for my IFFM wrap-up."

**AT:** And I think for the column, I transcribed that conversation.

**KS:** Phone rang another hour later and it was Peter Broderick, who wrote for *Filmmaker* magazine. And I knew him because we used that article. I was like, "What? Peter Broderick?" I was getting called by the indie all-stars. Peter Broderick's like, "At the behest of somebody who I really trust, I went into the video library and watched *Clerks*." 'Cause at the IFFM, you get a screening [and] you also gave them a tape, so people who couldn't make the screening could watch it in the video library. I was like, "Get out. Who is this person, man?"

He was like, "Well, you don't know him?"

I was like, "No."

He was like, "His name is Bob Hawk."

# JOHN PIERSON

**Kevin Smith:** Bob Hawk was like, "You gotta get this to John Pierson. He's trying to get out of the indie-film-repping business. Get this to John Pierson, man. He'll go crazy."

And I sent it to him. Nice letter and stuff. And I heard from Janet Pierson, his wife, who now runs South by Southwest Film Festival. And she was like, "He's out of town. He's coming back. But I dug it. I'm going to pass it on to him." And they told me [that] when he came home, she was like, "If you're truly out of the indie-film-repping business, don't watch *Clerks.*"

Kevin with John and Janet Pierson, from the *Spike, Mike, Slackers & Dykes* Premiere Party, Dolly's Books, Park City, Utah, 1996. *Courtesy of Janet Pierson*

# REPPING THE FILM

**John Pierson** [*on phone message*]: "Hey Kevin. John Pierson calling. Isn't this interesting? There were three Kevins who called in a row, you being number one in my book. I look forward to talking to you about *Clerks*, which I've seen twice. Okay. Bye."

**Kevin Smith:** And the phone call was pretty much this truncated, "Watched the movie. Think it's really funny, man. Don't think the audience for this movie exists yet, so I don't know if there's a marketplace for it. But if you're ever in the city, I'm happy to buy you lunch." And I was just like, "Oh, man."

**JP:** It wasn't, "Better luck next time." It wasn't quite like that. But it was sort of like, "That's it for now. We're putting you on the stack."

**JP** [*on phone message*]: "Kevin. John Pierson. Friday afternoon, 4:00. I watched your film yet again today, which must mean something. I'm hooked. I'm an addict. What can I tell you?"

**JP:** All I know is that for a week, I watched *Clerks* a lot. I'd reevaluated. But I probably called and said, "I guess it's inevitable. We're going to do this, so let's just get cooking."

# THE ENDING

**Bob Hawk:** In the original, Dante is shot dead at the end.

**John Willyung** [Kevin's cousin]: I don't even ask anything. I don't even say anything. I think my name is Quiet Man. If you look in the credit, it says, "Quiet Man." So I go in and I shoot Dante.

**Kevin Smith:** The movie's always been structurally based on *Do the Right Thing*, which happens over the course of the day. It's very funny, but then something very serious happens at the end. And then the movie concludes.

**Brian O'Halloran:** I hated it. Hated it. Hated it. Hated it. Hated it. I was like, "What? No!"

**BH:** And after falling in love with the film and then having this in the last few seconds of the film, one of the things I had to say right away is, "You can't kill Dante at the end. That has to go."

**John Pierson** [*on phone message*]: "Kevin. John Pierson. Friday afternoon, 4:00. I have an idea for you vis-à-vis your ending. Please call me. Bye."

**KS:** Pierson was the guy that really brought it all home. Pierson was like, "Look, you gotta lop that ending off."

**SM:** "You can't kill him at the end."

**KS:** "You kill the dude at the end for no better reason than you just don't know how to end your movie."

**JP:** I'm proud to say that I might have not been the first one to think it, but I was the first one to say, "Look. This ending's a problem."

**KS:** So he was like, "You can just end it without that. End it when his friend Randal leaves the store."

# HARVEY WALKS OUT

**Jon Gordon** [assistant to Harvey Weinstein]: Mark [Tusk, Miramax acquisitions], at the time, was trying to rally support for the film.

**Mark Tusk:** Rounded up friends, my brother, a few Miramax executives and more youthful staff . . .

**JG:** And Mark had set the screening up in order to show Harvey how the movie played with an audience.

**Kevin Smith:** Harvey, of course, was not the Harvey he is today. Now Harvey is synonymous with film in general, not just indie film. But I knew he was the head of Miramax, him and his brother ran Miramax.

**MT:** Harvey Weinstein was at the screening and Trea [Hoving], head of acquisitions.

**John Pierson:** A 16mm screening in the screening room at the Tribeca Film building.

**MT:** Harvey, of course, was an avid cigarette smoker. And so I'm not sure the smoking tirade at the beginning of the movie really drew him into it.

**JP:** The good news was great. All the young Miramaxers loved the movie.

**JG:** I loved it. For me, at that time, I was twenty-three years old. So that movie was speaking directly to me.

**JP:** But it was trumped by the bad news that Harvey walked out in fifteen minutes.

# SUBMITTING TO SUNDANCE

Kevin's career is inextricably intertwined with Harvey Weinstein, whom many consider the godfather of independent film. This photo was taken much later, at the premiere for *Zack and Miri Make a Porno* in 2008.
*AP Photo / Matt Sayles*

Since Weinstein's arrest and conviction for rape and sexual assault in 2020, Kevin has committed to donating residuals from his films made with Weinstein to Woman in Film, a nonprofit organization that supports women filmmakers.

**Kevin Smith:** There was no thought to go to Sundance until people started going, "Oh, you should definitely submit." And Bob Hawk, I finally got to talk to him, and he's like, "I'm very influential with the committee. I talk to them all the time. I tell them my picks. You have to submit this movie. This is a Sundance movie."

And I was like, "There's no stars in it. It's not in color."

He's like, "That doesn't matter. This is everything that festival's about." So it never occurred to me to go to Sundance until Hawk was like, "You gotta submit."

And it came down to the wire. It was split. The selection committee—half of them really loved it, half of them really didn't. Half of the half that didn't thought it was very misogynist, which I still can't see to this day. But it was Jason being like, "What's up, sluts?" out in front of the store. The Jason character was pretty much the lightning rod. And then Hawk called me at the store and he was like, "It's not written in stone, but it's looking good. There's a lot of pushback, but I think it might happen. I'll let you know for sure. But so far, no." And then he called me a half an hour later and he was like, "It's in! It's in!"

And I was like, "Ahhh!"

# KEEPING HOPE ALIVE

**Kevin Smith:** Nobody was picking us up. Our movie was just there to screen at Sundance.

**Scott Mosier:** Just for clarity, the only underlying thing was a few places, like Sony, were like, "Well, let's see how it plays."

**KS:** A wait-and-see kind of thing.

**SM:** Basically, everyone had passed. But everyone had sort of said, "Wait and see how it plays," which wasn't really a big pile of hope to stand on.

# NEWS FROM THE FRONT LINES

**Kevin Smith** [*reading his journal*]: "Scott comes back from dropping off Kristin [his sister] in town to report that he talked to John Pierson and got two interesting pieces of info. One, the head *Variety* critic, Todd McCarthy, loved *Clerks*. He was at the first screening, as well as J. Hoberman and Dave Kehr." J. Hoberman wrote for the *Village Voice*, and Dave Kehr, I think, was the *Daily News* . . .

**Scott Mosier:** Think about that. Think about 1994, how people communicated.

**KS:** Isn't that strange?

**SM:** It wasn't like John could text or call or whatever. It was all done by foot. Footman.

**KS:** It was literally like being in the Civil War. Scott ran with a message, ducking buckshot and musket fire, and finally reached me and was like, [*panting with a British accent*] "Lead critic of *Variety* . . ."

**SM** [*imitates British accent*]: "Word from Pierson."

**KS:** It's true, man. Now you'd fuckin' sign on to the Internet . . .

**SM:** Or even if he did get advance personally, he would call, cell phones or whatever.

**KS:** Or text you right away.

**SM:** I think I randomly ran into him, and so that was the way to get the information, 'cause I was actually there. Otherwise, we would have waited.

**KS:** Isn't that nuts? [*Continues reading his journal*] "Describing it as fuckin' hilarious," he said. And two, Trea is now full throttle on *Clerks*' side after gauging audience reaction to the morning screening. So Trea, [who] was just like, "I don't know," was now like, "Yeah, man. This could work." So she's on [Mark] Tusk's side.

# DAVE KEHR REVIEW

**Kevin Smith** [*reading his journal*]: "John also related Dave Kehr's *Daily News* piece, which calls *Clerks* 'a cross between Howard Stern and David Mamet.'" Now to say that, that could've been it. I could've went home. Somebody, anybody referencing Howard Stern and David Mamet. Drop the mike, ladies and gentlemen. That's fuckin' the best thing you could possibly say about me.

# FINAL SUNDANCE SCREENING

Kevin at the Sundance Film Festival, Park City, Utah, 1994
*Courtesy of Sandria Miller*

**Jeff Anderson:** Sure enough, Harvey [Weinstein] walks in, and he's walking down the aisle and it got quiet, and then there was a little buzz, like, "Harvey's here. Harvey's here. Harvey's here."

**Harvey Weinstein:** We ended up being pushed into a screening, and [Mark] Tusk was sitting on one side of me, and I think he put someone else on the other side of me. I couldn't leave.

*Introduction is from the Sundance screening recorded at the Egyptian Theatre in 1994.*

**Geoffrey Gilmore:** To introduce the film to you, with great pleasure, Kevin Smith . . .

**Kevin Smith:** It was a really nice intro, but the rags part, I believe. The riches part have not come, so we're still waiting. I just want to thank everyone for coming out tonight. This is our last screening, so it means a lot to us, and we've had a great time. It's been a great eight days thus far, and we've still got two more to go. The food's been free. You can't ask for anything more. We've gotten some great press. The interesting thing I heard, though, is that the *Convenience Store News* just called today and wants to do a cover story on us. Afterwards, we're going to bring up the actors. You can meet the people who were involved and the tech crew and stuff like that. But while I'm here, I just want to thank a few people. Mr. Gilmore, of course. Bob Hawk, kind of our angel. John Pierson. Tusk. Anyone else I might have forgotten. So that's it. Let's roll. And enjoy, please.

**Mark Tusk:** Harvey was squirming again in the first ten minutes of the movie. I nudged him and said, "37" [a reference to blow jobs].

**KS:** Tusk yanked him back down in the seat and was like, "You just sit here and think '37.'"

**MT:** "Until you hear the word '37,' you can't leave yet."

**KS:** Once the "37" scene kicked in, there was one dude who was boisterously laughing throughout the flick. Like Bob De Niro in *Cape Fear.* Like "Ah-ha-ha-ha-ha." Like, really laughing loud. We're like, "Who the fuck is that? What an annoying laugh. So distracting." It was Harvey.

**MT:** Soon enough, he was laughing uproariously. Probably louder than most people in the theater.

**John Pierson:** You could literally hear him in the movie theater. It was great.

**Brian O'Halloran:** I was just like, "Wow, wow . . ."

**KS** [*reading his journal*]: "The crowd eats it up. There is louder, longer laughter than at any of the previous screenings. When Silent Bob delivers his single line, there are cheers and claps. It ends. Big fucking applause. I get up and bring the cast with me. We do a bit of Q&A."

**Jon Gordon:** Harvey exited at the far-right door of the Egyptian Theatre as the throngs were coming out. He came out of the theater and he picked his head up and went [*thumbs-up gesture*], like that.

**MT:** We went to a place across the street from the Egyptian.

**KS:** The Eating Establishment. That's what it was called.

**Scott Mosier:** From the moment you heard, it was like, "Something's happening. Something's happening that we can't understand or contemplate, 'cause we've never been in these circumstances. Something's happening."

**KS:** We sit down with Harvey Weinstein.

**MT:** We ordered some potato skins with bacon.

**JP:** He was both going to eat and sign off on the fundamental terms of the deal at the same time.

**HW:** Buy the movie on the spot and just make a deal with him over potato skins and french fries at some Sundance restaurant.

**BH:** I was in the room. I was in this same large room at this restaurant, and I knew what was going on. I couldn't wait to find out.

**MT:** Harvey did his song and dance, as far as how much he loved the movie.

**HW:** They all liked it, you know what I mean? It was me who was just being stupid. The rest of them were totally into it. Jon loved it. Tusk loved it. All the cool people at Miramax. It was just the old fart who couldn't get his head around it. And then I went to see it at that screening in Sundance and flipped.

**KS:** He was like, "Fuckin' loved the movie. Think it's really fuckin' funny. We take this fuckin' movie. Blow it out in fuckin' theaters. Put a fuckin' soundtrack on it. Take this movie to the fuckin' world." Me and [Mosier] were like, "Fuckin' A."

**HW:** And it taught me a lesson not to walk out of movies.

**MT:** By this point, everyone knew it cost 27,000 bucks.

**JP:** A really fair advance would be a couple hundred thousand, plus let's throw in the 27 for what actually got spent on the film. Let's make it 227 and just make it simple and sweet.

**KS:** John Pierson was like, "Let's go." And so he pulled me and Scott to the side and he was like, "All right. This is the moment. We all know why we're here, and we know we didn't get into this to make money. I think I speak for you guys when I'm saying, 'It doesn't matter how much they're offering us.'" He's going, "I think what they're offering us is fine. I really don't think we should push them and ask for more."

I was like, "I don't give a shit about money. I want to see Miramax at the head of this film. That would be fuckin' phenomenal. I don't give a shit if they give us no money."

**HW:** It really was thanks to Mark Tusk and his incredible persistence that the rest is history. I'm buying this movie.

**MT:** Harvey signed off on the deal.

**KS:** Harvey was like, "Excellent to meet you. Can't wait to work with you. [*Sound of rushing wind*] And he was gone. And Tusk the whole time was sitting there. And we would look at Tusk and Tusk was nodding yes. And we were like, "Yes!"

**KS** [*reading his journal*]: "What seemed almost impossible came to pass. Miramax bought *Clerks*!"

Scott Finnis | New York |
"Dante & Veronica from *Clerks*," 2014

# TRIMS

**Kevin Smith:** We were cutting on 16mm workprint. So, back in the day, you would take trims, selects, hang 'em up from a bin and shit, little paper clips in their sprocket holes hanging over this bin, and pull out all your shots that you were gonna use. The rest, all these hundreds of feet of workprint—which you were never going to use, all wasted material—we threw in massive garbage bags and put in the back of RST Video.

And we sold it to Miramax, and Harvey Weinstein was like, "You gotta cut ten minutes." He was like, "I don't know what to cut. You're a young man. It's a young man's movie. Figure out ten minutes to cut."

So we go looking for the time and we go, "All right, let's go back to the editing room," which was RST Video. We looked at the bags of footage to look for material to cut with. Cut away from a shot to another shot. But we didn't shoot *Clerks* with a shit ton of coverage. And we looked at all those big bags and I was like, "You know what, man. Fuck it. Let's just trim without it." And we never went back. Who knows what fuckin' material lies in there. There's a whole different version of the movie, but we couldn't because it was too daunting seeing all that workprint.

# DISTRIBUTION

**Kevin Smith:** Me and Mosier went to sit down with Harvey Weinstein in his office. The dude's like a cartoon octopus. Hands going everywhere: cutting a movie here, smoking a cigar here, drinking a Diet Coke here, yelling at his assistant with this hand, looking at a poster concept. He was amazing. I didn't even know if he knew we were sitting there. He goes, "Listen, storytelling, making movies is this simple. The movie doesn't begin and end when the audience gets into the theater. If you're good at your job, the movie begins for them long before they fuckin' left their houses. And if you're a magician, the movie never ends, even when the credits roll. It just keeps going."

Todd Slater | Austin, Texas |
"*Clerks*," 2006

Justin McFarland | Los Angeles, California | *"Clerks* movie poster," 2012

Blake Wheeler | Charleston, West Virginia | "quickcast & ratscast," 2011

# MALLRATS

1995

# REBELLION

**FOR HIS NEXT FILM,** Kevin Smith chose the mall as metaphor. A communal meeting place. A celebration of capitalism. An escape from home. Somewhere to hang with your crew, meet girls, act stupid, and give the middle finger to the corporate assholes. It's about growing up and maybe getting your shit together. It speaks to a generation of kids who were trying to figure things out and accepting the fact that it was time to move out of their parents' house. This applied to Kevin as well. He was starting his own life, believing he could do whatever he wanted. When you're young, it's all possible. You can make the money, get the girl, and still stick it to the man. He had started out as a clerk but found himself in the mall.

Initially, the audience didn't support the film in theaters. However, because of its long tail on home video, the fans ended up giving it a life on VHS and DVD. It was those kids, like the ones in the film, who were still hanging out at the mall, going to the movies, eating in the food court, and playing video games. Those fans were the post-high-school grads without helicopter parents, living a perpetual adolescence and never really wanting to grow up.

# JIM JACKS

**Kevin Smith:** When me and Mos wound up going out to Hollywood, doing the business rounds, we were flown out by Hollywood Pictures to meet with them. We met with a bunch of people. But one of the people we wanted to meet with, I kept saying, "Jim Jacks. He seemed to really like us. He wanted to buy *Clerks*, so maybe we can go in there. And it's at Universal. And Universal was the home of *Breakfast Club* and *Do the Right Thing*, one of my favorite movies of all time, and *The Blues Brothers* and *Jaws*." That's where their deal was set up.

When we came out to Hollywood, we met with Jim and Sean [Daniel, head of Alphaville Films]; and after we talked about meeting with other people and talked about movies we saw: "What do you want to do next?"

And I was like, "I don't know. We were talking about doing this movie called *Mallrats*."

"I love that. What is it?"

And I was like, "*Clerks* in a mall."

And he goes, "Perfect." So from that moment forward, [he was] the most enthusiastic—honestly, more enthusiastic than us.

I wanted to make *Dogma*, but I knew I couldn't make it next. And so I was like, "This is great. I could make a movie here. A studio movie. I'll make a studio version of *Clerks*." So I say, "*Mallrats*," and boom! It just starts moving forward. But Jim loved the idea so

much, he breathed life into it. Immediately took us to the black tower [Universal corporate offices], remember? Pitch it to Casey Silver and Nina Jacobson. So Jim is in every way, shape, and form the godfather of *Mallrats*. Nobody else in town was angling to make *Mallrats*. To be fair, we never sent it to anybody but them. But who knows if it ever would have been made? Now maybe it's easier to say, of course—but 1994–95, they weren't making R-rated comedies anymore. That genre, teen-titty comedy, was gone and dead. They didn't make movies like that. *Clueless* came out the same year as *Mallrats*. And that's a PG-13 movie. So you get a lot of "balls going past your nose" jokes, but nobody's saying, "Fuck." Nobody's cursing, talking about sex or something like that. It's all *Dating Game*–style, whoopee-type jokes.

So Jim loved that, though. He's like, "I'll make a *Porky's*." He was the one who coined the phrase "a smart *Porky's*."

**Kevin Smith:** You needed two bankable names, names [the studio] felt were bankable enough to hang a marketing campaign on before they would even think about giving you a greenlight. So Shannen Doherty was a get for us, man. They were like, "That's fantastic!" She just got off *90210* and stuff, had a lot of press, so that definitely rang their greenlight. It worked out for us 'cause she was good. She's a real good actress. She's fast. She's funny. And then on the other side, we needed one more, and we couldn't pull one. We wanted Jason Lee really badly, and there was another guy that they kinda liked who had more TV exposure. But we loved Jason. He was original and different. Not the obvious choice.

So we had to figure out a way to kinda give them what they wanted in the other direction, and it wound up being Jeremy London, the guy who played T.S. [He] was on a very critically hailed show called *I'll Fly Away*, which had no ratings whatsoever.

And because he was on that show, though, and we could point to, like, "Oh, the critics all like it," the studio was like, "Okay, there you go. That's fine with us."

"Whew!" 'Cause he was also who we felt, at the time, was the right man for the job.

Shannen Doherty as Rene, Jason Lee as Brodie, and Kevin directing, 1995
*AF Archive / Universal / Alamy Stock Photo*

# JASON LEE

**Kevin Smith** [*speaking to actor Jason Lee*]: I discovered this guy, kind of. Really, the credit goes to Don Phillips, an amazing casting director who cast *Fast Times at Ridgemont High*, *Dazed and Confused*, and then he also cast *Mallrats*. And Jason was somebody he brought in. And before you were an actor, when we were sitting there talking about the pages before the audition, I said, "So what have you been doing prior to this?"

And he goes, "I just retired."

And I said, "Retired?" He was like twenty-one or something like that. I said, "What'd you retire from?"

And he said, "Professional skateboarding."

And I was like, "You used to skateboard?"

And he was like, "I retired from professional skateboarding."

You were ollieing things?

**Jason Lee**: It was something I did my whole life, and then I turned pro in the late '80s and then somehow wanted to become an actor.

**KS**: When you came in and read, this is what put you above everybody else. There's a line that's not even in the movie anymore. It's in the cut sequences, like all the cut footage on the DVD, if you see it. But at one point, Brodie has to say the term "black mass." He's talking about,

"I saw my neighbors at a blaaack maaass." And that's how you say black mass. Jason Lee, when he read it, he would be like, "Blaaack maaass." He held out his a's. And everyone comes through on auditions and you're reading along with them, and sometimes you're looking at them and stuff. Sometimes you're looking down to the next line. And all of a sudden, I hear him going, "Blaaack maaass," and I snapped up 'cause I was like, "That was different."

**JL**: I was terrible then.

**KS**: No. It's not that it was terrible. It was different. We developed a way to communicate with one another in directing that some people would be like, "It's ridiculous. It's ludicrous," but it really worked for us. If you watch *Mallrats*, there's points when Jason does kind of lyrical dialogue. One is like, "It's not a mall; it's the mall. Show some respect . . ."

**JL**: Oh, "A small price to pay for the smiting . . . of one's enemies."

**KS**: Yes. Yes. That became the "Brodie." And in order to get there, I was trying to explain how you were climbing and then descending, 'cause he did it in real life. And I picked it up one day. I was like, "Do that. Do that thing you do." He was like, "What thing?" And I was like, "This thing. Do like this [*hand rising and falling with dialogue*]: 'Smiting . . . of one's enemies.'" And he's like, "What is that?" And I'm like, "This? [*hand rising and falling*] This is how you should talk." It was magical.

**Kevin Smith** [*speaking to actor Jason Mewes*]: They didn't let you be in the cast at first. We were going through the cast of the movie. They were like, "Okay, Jay is a great part. Who's gonna play that?"

And I was like, "Jay. Jason Mewes. The guy who played him in *Clerks*."

And they're like, "Well, we're thinking of putting an actor in that, 'cause that's a really funny part."

And I was like, "Yeah, but it's Mewes. It's Jay. Jay plays Jay. Jay is Jay. You know, it's not so much a part as kinda that guy."

So we brought Mewes out, and Mewes had to audition. Mewes came in and fuckin' turned it up, really gave a phenomenal audition. I was like, "I don't think anybody in this room can fight me on Jason Mewes anymore."

And still, they were like, "Okay. Well, how 'bout this? We'll let you shoot with him for one week and if we like the dailies, fine. But if we don't like the dailies, we're going to fire him and bring out either Seth Green or Breckin Meyer to reshoot all that stuff, and they'll be Jay at that point."

So I had to fly Mewes out, and then Mewes slept on my floor for all of preproduction, right up to the first week of shooting, because the first week of shooting was all about passing muster. But [Mewes] crushed it, and by the end of the first day, even [producer] Jim Jacks was like, "I'm talking to the studio, man. That kid's gold. He ain't gotta fuckin' worry about it. He's in the movie."

I went and told Mewes, "Dude, congratulations, man. You crushed it. They're gonna fuckin' let you be in the movie."

And he was like, "Awesome."

I was like, "That means you get to move into your own room," and he got all fuckin' quiet. And I was like, "You don't want to leave my room, do you?"

And he was like, "No. We play video games in here." So he fuckin' lived in my room for the rest of the fuckin' show. And every day I'd wake up, go take a shower; he'd say, "Me first, Moves," and run into the bathroom and fuckin' use up the hot water and shit like that. Such a bitch.

"Mewes at 'Build Me Up Buttercup'
video shoot, circa 1995."
—Kevin Smith

# TEST SCREENINGS

**Kevin Smith:** San Diego. First time I was here, or in this neck of the woods, was in support of *Mallrats*. We'd shot *Mallrats* and we were going to come down here to show it. And it made sense. It was a very comic-book-oriented film, and Comic-Con was happening. So we came down. We showed it at the Horton Plaza, that movie theater. It was probably hands-down the best screening of anything we've ever done, ever. It was religious, man. It was almost as if we were showing those fuckin' Mel Gibson fans another movie where Jesus gets the shit beat out of him. Plays through the roof, man. Through the roof.

So we came down here with *Jay and Silent Bob Strike Back*. Bob's like [*imitates Bob Weinstein's New York accent*], "We're going to test the movie."

I was like, "Bob, you can't test a movie called *Jay and Silent Bob Strike Back*. The only people interested in this movie are going to be View Askew fans, Jay and Silent Bob fans. So maybe we should test with just them."

And he's like, "No. We gotta have a regular mainstream test to see if other people want to come see your movie."

So I said, "Well, can I pick where it plays?" He goes, "Yeah, go ahead." And I said, "San Diego." And he goes, "Okay. Why San Diego?" And I said, "You can drive there from Los Angeles. And we had a test screening there; it was good. Comic-Con's down there. It was a good cross section."

You start throwing out buzz words. We tested *Jersey Girl* here once too, and they wouldn't count the scores 'cause they were good. Bob Weinstein was like, "I'm wise to you, Kevin."

And I was like, "What do you mean?"

"San Diego is ruined for us." He literally goes, "Too many people in San Diego like your movies."

And I was like, "So then, why is that a skewed test?"

And he's like, "Because it's not going to be like that anywhere else in the world."

And he was fuckin' right.

"Back in 1995, this badge would've gotten you into the *Mallrats* premiere party, which was held at B.B. King."
—Kevin Smith

**Kevin Smith:** The other night, I thought I'd do a fun experiment where I would smoke weed and try to watch *Mallrats*. Here we go [*reading from notes*], "Opening scene would be so much better if, to apologize, T.S. started to quietly but intensely eat Brandi's pussy."

**Scott Mosier:** It certainly would have been more fun to shoot.

**KS:** And then I added, "Right there in the driveway. Or even better, while he's doing it, we angle up on his face in ecstasy and see a dragon in the sky."

**SM:** I'm ready to go back into Universal right now, and we're like, "You can't tell me this isn't going to make money!"

**KS:** I was trying to figure it out, like, "Dragons?" My sister's got two kids. Her daughter Sabine is a bit autistic, but she's very focused autistic. She sent me an email earlier that day. Just a one-line email. It says, "I have an idea for a movie about a girl dragon who has an adventure in the city."

**SM:** I don't think that's her version.

**KS:** I want to write her back and be like, "How's this sound?"

# MALLRATS SEQUEL

**Kevin Smith** [*reading from notes*]: "Brodie really believes in the mall. He'd be heartbroken now, as malls lie dying across America." I pitch a sequel. "A *Mallrats* sequel would be about how Brodie tries to save the Eden Prairie Mall from economic collapse. He tries to convince the government that the Eden Prairie Mall is so large, they can't let it fail. Movie would open with Brodie getting out of jail after six months' time for hacking into amazon.com and posting a message like Anonymous did with the Westboro Baptist website. The message urges fat America to stop button-pushing shopping and start mall-walking again."

**Scott Mosier:** So that becomes his call to arms?

**KS:** That's before the movie even opens. It opens kind of like *Cape Fear*, with him getting out of jail after six months for trying to fuckin' bring up real-life commerce as opposed to e-commerce. But apparently

that's not enough. By act three, it all concludes with Brodie throwing a pajama jammy-jam to save the mall—the mother of all house parties.

**SM:** I knew there was going to be a *House Party* moment in there at some point.

**KS:** I'm telling you, dude. This is fuckin' making me rethink retirement. I'm like, "This movie should happen, man." *Mallrats* with dragons, and they got a *House Party* dance going on.

*Opposite:* Salvador Anguiano | Irapuato, Mexico | "*Mallrats* - Alternative movie poster," 2015

"This poster is really a love letter to one of my favorite movies ever. I dig Kevin Smith, love his movies, hear his podcast, watch *Comic Book Men*, read one of his books, and usually try to catch his talks on YouTube, you get it, I'm a fan. The guy seems to genuinely love and care for his fans, and that is enough to put him at the top of my list, but he also is a talented, smart guy, so additional points to his ranking!"

—Salvador Anguiano

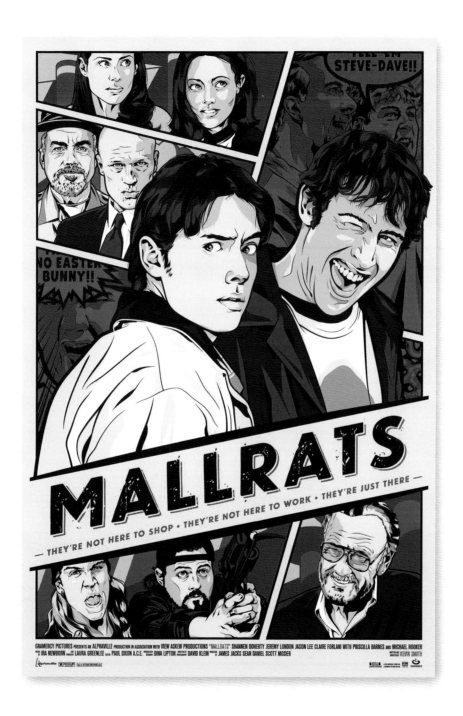

# CHASING AMY

1997

# BUILDING THE RELATIONSHIP

**KEVIN SMITH DECIDED TO** make his third film about friendships interfering with love, the difficulties of living on the sexual spectrum, and how growing up means leaving childhood behind. As he grew as a filmmaker, he moved away from his past films. The challenge was finding new ways to tell stories and facing his own fears of intimacy. This decision speaks to how Kevin finally understood that creativity is more than making stuff up. It's about sharing and giving up the person he used to be and realizing he could never go back to the past.

Kevin's fans embraced the film, and one of the reasons was because Kevin opened up about his love for comics. The fans saw that he was not ashamed to say he was a huge comics nerd. Although this type of character is typically thought of as socially awkward, someone who has difficulty seeking out meaningful relationships, Kevin revealed some heavy, emotional stuff about his lack of sexual experience and a partner who was more adventurous than he was. Fans also responded to Kevin's casting of the young and up-and-coming Ben Affleck, someone whom Kevin thought could be a leading man.

# MOVIE JAIL

**Kevin Smith:** Let me set the stage for you, man. At the time we made this movie, we were done. Like, finished. Movie jail. *Clerks* had done well for an independent film. *Mallrats* we made for $6 million, and it grossed $2 million in the States. I don't think they even released it overseas. So we were done. Nobody was fuckin' looking for anything from us ever again. And so we were working from a great place creatively. No expectations, man. You can kind of go in there and rock their socks off. Or at least try to rock their socks off.

# SCOTT HEARS THE NEWS

**Kevin Smith:** I called [Scott Mosier] from Sundance. "I sat down with Harvey Weinstein," I said. "I got the budget."

And he goes, "How d'you do that?"

And I said, "'Cause I'm that good. I've got a silver tongue."

**Scott Mosier:** The budget . . . which was a million.

**KS:** You were looking for a million bucks. And then you were like, "Great. And how much?" I was like, "He even gave us more money for the actors."

You're like, "Get outta here!"

"Yeah. He gave us 50,000 additional bucks." And he goes, "So, what . . . like, a million fifty thousand is our budget?" I was like, "No, dude: $250,000."

And then there was silence.

# PITCHING MIRAMAX

**Kevin Smith:** "Here's my script, and I'm gonna do it with my friends. I'm gonna do it with Ben Affleck, Joey Adams, Jason Lee."

I literally was told, "This job isn't about making movies with your friends, Kevin. It's a job. It's work. There's money."

So I was like, "Well, who do you guys see?"

And they're like, "We have deals with three people that'd be wonderful for this. Drew Barrymore, Jon Stewart, and David Schwimmer." And this is Jon Stewart pre-*The Daily Show*, 1996.

So I'm like, "That's great. I've seen them all in stuff. I know they're legit. I don't think they suck, but I didn't write this movie with those cats in mind, and I don't have any interest in seeing that version of the movie, really. If I'm gonna make it, I'm gonna live and die by my cats." So we went from a $3 million budget to a $200,000 budget by virtue of the fact that I was like, "Look, if I do it with my friends for $200K, you guys have first crack at it if you pay for it. And if you don't like it, let us go sell it."

And Harvey Weinstein was like, "I'll give you fifty more thousand to pay the cast, so you can do it for $250K."

I thought that was so generous, and then I figured out years later, "If I pay for the cast now, I won't have to pay 'em later. I'll own this thing outright." And he did. He got a very inexpensive movie, $250K, that they wound up making $12 million at the box office. And that was because I was like, "I want this cast so badly." For me, and I don't advocate this for anybody else, but for me, I've always made the fuckin' stupid choice to get what I want. But I've always felt, "I'll die on the sword on this." I'm just like, "Look, I'd rather go do this by myself than take your money to do it in a way that just doesn't seem right."

# SECRET ORIGINS

**Kevin Smith** [*speaking to producer Scott Mosier*]: Joey Adams. Phenomenal job in this movie. We were dating at the time that we made this movie. I mean, I wrote this movie for her. It was about our relationship, kind of. Guin Turner and Mosier are the origin for this movie, 'cause Guin Turner was the chick who wrote *Go Fish*. We met her and Rose Troche at Sundance. Mos and Guin started hanging out more and more. And I was always like, "It's so fruitless to like somebody who's like, 'You don't have what I need.'" So that was the beginning. That's when I started thinking about it.

**Scott Mosier:** You were like, "You should write this."

**KS:** I gave it to Mos first. I remember literally saying at one point, "Either you write or I'm gonna." You were too busy trying to tag Guin Turner. You were like, "I'm too busy, man. I got shit going on over here." So I was like, "I'm gonna write it." Joey was the secondary influence. 'Cause when I first thought about writing it, it was just the superficial idea 'cause you'd been hanging out with Guin since '94 through '95 and I wrote this in '96.

When I was talking about doing it with Jim Jacks [in '95], he was like, "What do you want to do next?"

While we were on *Mallrats* post, I said, "I want to make this movie about this guy who falls in love with a lesbian."

He goes, "Oh, man. Set it in high school."

I said, "Really?"

He goes, "*Clueless* made so much money."

And then *Mallrats* died. So I was like, "Does anybody still want the high school lesbian movie? Hello? I didn't think so." So I was able to be like, "I'm gonna write [it]."

Kevin and Joey Lauren Adams attend the premiere of *Chasing Amy*, 1997. *Kathy Hutchins / ZUMA Press, Inc. / Alamy Stock Photo*

Kevin, Scott Mosier, and Rose Troche at Sundance, 1994 *Courtesy of Sandria Miller*

# BEN'S IMPROV

**Kevin Smith:** [Affleck] would fuckin' add dialogue. We were doing the swing-set scene and he's sitting there and Alyssa is describing fisting. And so, he fuckin' reacts. He's just like, "Oh my God, does it hurt?"

And she goes, "We only do it once in a while. It's reserved for special occasions." And the line he's supposed to say in the script is, "What do you do for not-so-special occasions?" And then she goes on, fuckin' says something else.

So we're shooting it, and I'm like, "Action!"

I'm sitting behind the monitor, got my headphones on, and you hear the line; she does this [*imitates fisting*], puts her hand through, and he reacts. I'm looking at the monitor and she goes, "We only do it once in a while. It's reserved for special occasions."

And then Affleck goes, "Jesus, what do you do for not-so-special occasions?" He goes, "Hit her in the head with a fuckin' bat?"

And I was sitting there listening. I was like,. "That's not in the script, man." I was like, "Cut!" I walked over and was like, "What the fuck, dude?"

He was like, "Do you like that shit, man?"

I was like, "Not at all. You really ruined a tender moment."

He was like, "Tender? You're talking about fisting, man." He was going, "I threw that in for my peeps." This is 1996. He had no peeps whatsoever.

So I said, "Dude, do me a favor? Fuckin' keep your dialogue out of my movie. This is my movie, my dialogue. You wanna write dialogue, go write it in your own script. Make your own movie." And he did, and he won a fuckin' Academy Award.

Kevin directing Ben Affleck as Holden, 1997
*AF Archive / Miramax / Alamy Stock Photo*

# EDITING ON AVID

**Kevin Smith:** Going into *Chasing Amy*, Mosier was like, "Hey, man, let's cut digitally. We'll cut Avid [a nonlinear editing software]."

And I said, "Okay. But how do we do that?"

"I'm gonna go take a class. And I'll cut."

"Great. I'll sit behind and I'll tell you what to cut and shit," 'cause I couldn't get my head around using a computer. So we sit down for the first day to edit, and Mosier's sitting at the deck. And watching someone edit when you have an editor's soul is like watching someone play a video game. It's frustrating 'cause you're like, "Go. Go over. Do this. Give me the controller. All right. Here. Now go. Oh, you fucked it up again. Give me this." So I sat behind Mosier for a good two hours going, like, "Move that over here. Move that shot over. Just move. Here. Give me this. Let me see. How do you do it? You click on this? Drag this? All right. Let me try this. Okay. That's what I'm talking about."

And he's like, "Oh, you know how to do it now."

And I was like, "No, no. You do it, man." And I'd sit behind him, and again I'd be like, "Fuck it. No. Pull this thing over. You're missing it. Give me the controls."

And finally, within an hour, I got the hang of it and he was there to be like, "Press this button." Mosier will tell you, "I used to like editing too, and then Kevin took over. And then I just sat there to be like, 'Press A.'" And that's not really editing. That's like being an assistant. So on *Clerks II*, I was like, "I know it's frustrating to sit next to me and not edit while I'm editing, so you don't have to sit there. I'll just cut myself."

And he was like, "Okay, bye." Fucked off. So it was a little frustrating, I guess.

On Avid, man, if you wanna try anything, you can cut a version of the movie, and fuckin' cut a completely different version of the movie, and then just be like, "Throw it out, doesn't matter." It's so easy. All the stuff's there. So because of that, you make better choices or different choices. So, as I was cutting *Chasing Amy*, I was like, "Let me use this, man. Let me go to a blown take that just had one line that was totally usable. If I can fish that out, that'll be genius." So I would do that as well. I would look at everything. Back in the day, you would do circle takes and be like, "We just print a certain amount." But I was like, "Print everything. Just dump it into the Avid. Don't print it. Load everything into the Avid." That way, even if there's something that did nothing, a terrible take for like ten minutes, if I got one line, it's gonna be gold. Even if I find that one line, I can save the scene.

Kevin and Joey Lauren Adams at the monitor, 1997. *Courtesy of Lorenzo Bevilaqua*

# EMERSON SCREENING

**Kevin Smith:** I came to speak at Emerson [College, in Boston], and it was one of the first places where I spoke very frankly and very candidly about the failure of *Mallrats*. I brought in a scene and showed them stuff and talked about the marketing, where I started being honest. It started at Emerson. So I'm talking very passionately about *Mallrats* and failure and working within the system. I threw up a scene from *Chasing Amy*. We had shot it, but the movie hadn't been out, yet. It wouldn't go to Sundance for another couple months. And so we ran the sequence where Ben and Joey are in the rain and he fuckin' tells her he loves her and shit, whole thing, him in the car . . .

**Jason Mewes:** I cried at that part.

**KS:** Did you really? [*imitating Mewes*] "This is as beautiful as [the TV show] *Charmed*. You reached a *Charmed* level, Kev." So he does his whole "I love you," and she gets out and he chases her in the rain. And it's that sequence—which, again, at that point, I had made *Clerks* and *Mallrats*, so that sequence is pretty fuckin' dope if you've never seen me do anything but those two movies. Like, "Oh, shit, this dude's got some depth, some shade, some color. He could go places other than him and the silly dude running around with their hands down their pants." So they're watching this sequence and you feel it in the room, people are like, "Oh shit!" And they're young, they're all fuckin' college kids and whatnot, and I'm still relatively young at that point. I was about twenty-six, twenty-seven. So that movie's right in the right moment, the right vibe, and this is before anybody gets to see it. You can feel it in the room. It's playing. This movie might work, 'cause we hadn't shown it to anybody yet.

And at the end of the sequence, the lights come up and everybody goes, "Whooo!" And we're like, "All right, right on, we got something here." And then I take a question. The dude stands up and he goes, "Hey, man, great scene. I just wanted to point out in case you didn't see it: when Ben is walking back to the car, you see your entire crew reflected in the window behind him."

And I was like, "What? What are you talking about? No." And I'd never seen that. I'd been working on the film, editing it on a much smaller screen, so I'd never really saw it projected big. So I rewound it, and we went and watched it again, because I was like, "This kid's out of his fuckin' mind." And I was like, "Holy fuck! That's the crew."

It seems like maybe three in ten people, if you talk about *Chasing Amy*, would be like, "Wonderful, wonderful movie. Hey, did you know that you can see the crew in the window?" I called up Affleck. I was like, "What do you think we should do? We might have to go with the other take, dude." And he goes, "No, no, no, no. No, that's the take. That's the take. That was the bomb take. Man, use that take." And I was like, "We got the people in the background reflected in the glass." He's just like, "Don't you fuckin' worry about it, dude. They'll be staring at Affleck."

And I'll give it up for him. Seven in ten people are staring at Ben Affleck. But three out of ten stare past him to be like, "Who are those ten people walking with Ben Affleck? These phantom hitchhiking ghosts in the window."

Scott Finnis | New York | "*Chasing Amy* the Manga," 2015

# DOGMA

1999

# SECULARISM VS. FAITH

**CATHOLICISM WAS SOMETHING THAT** Kevin Smith had wanted to talk about since he started making films. With his fourth film, the story of angels trying to get back to heaven was an opportunity to lambast sacred cows and show that the world had stopped caring about living a spiritual life. Nothing was sacred. By raising these questions, Kevin sparked outrage. Mixing humor and religion was a combustible combination, with strippers, drug dealers, poop monsters, and a fake Jesus populating one of the world's most venerable institutions. Kevin never wanted to crap on religion, nor did he want to be its savior.

Religion and politics are personal, and we know it. Any discussion will turn off lots of people. But there are many who appreciated Kevin for being risky. He didn't shy away from controversy, and he got plenty of it. People were protesting at the multiplex, and Kevin was getting death threats. In today's climate, political correctness probably would have killed it. But the fans were the ones who ultimately saved the movie. Kevin never went as far as Bill Maher's documentary *Religulous*, because he wasn't trying to be critical. He had his own struggles with religion but never lost faith in the film.

# TURNING IN THE SCRIPT

**Scott Mosier:** We were supposed to do *Dogma* [after *Mallrats*]. *Dogma* had been turned in.

**Kevin Smith:** Yeah. But I didn't want to do it. I kept putting off *Dogma*. That was me personally every step of the way, 'cause it was always a very relaxed process in terms of submitting stuff to Miramax. We submitted *Dogma* at the Toronto Film Festival in '94, which is the tail end of the festival year, 'cause we started with *Clerks* in January of '94. So then, almost a year later—September, October '94—we're at the Toronto Film Festival and I'd already handed in the *Dogma* script that week.

**SM:** We had to hand it in.

**KS:** We didn't end up making it for, like, four years at that point.

**SM:** We had to hand it in before we went to make *Mallrats*.

**KS:** They didn't care. Right before *Mallrats* came out, we had signed an overall deal with the Weinsteins. So they had us either way. We were there for the next movie. They didn't care what it was. But they were happy that it was gonna be cheap because *Dogma*, at that point, we were looking for three, four million bucks.

George Carlin as Cardinal Glick, 1998
*Photo by Darren Michaels, smpsp*

# ALAN RICKMAN

**Kevin Smith:** In 1997, we had this movie out, *Chasing Amy*. A friend of mine goes, "Hey, man. I just spoke to Alan Rickman, and Alan is a massive fuckin' *Chasing Amy* fan. He loved that movie."

And I was like, "Really? Are you shitting me? I love fuckin' Alan Rickman." They said, "Aren't you doing *Dogma*? Why don't you send him a script?"

So I sent him a script for *Dogma*, and he responded immediately. And this was a dude who, I was told when we sent him a script, they're like, "Don't expect a yes. He's fuckin' insanely picky."

So when he said yes, I was like, "He ain't that fuckin' picky, man. Holy shit." So he was the first non-friend to sign onto that movie. You know, Ben [Affleck], and fuckin' Matt [Damon] and Jason Lee and Jason Mewes, those guys were friends. He was the first one that wasn't a friend who kind of stepped up and said, "I like this quite a bit." And boy, did he fuckin' like it. He wasn't there the whole show, 'cause he was in a total of ten minutes of the movie. But his performance is so wonderful, you think he's in every fuckin' scene in the movie.

While he was there, we put this giant wings harness on him. He was actually wearing it. We had levers controlling it from another room. The wings were about 150 pounds on his back. And during the day of fuckin' opening them and closing them, we threw his back out in a big bad fuckin' way. And he still had to shoot the next day. And if you watch the movie, when he slides in at the table—they're at the restaurant, they're like, "What are we doing here?"—and he's like, "Going out in style." And that's when he's like, "I say we get drunk 'cause I'm all out of ideas." When he slides into that chair, that night he could not fuckin' stand or sit, he was in so much fuckin' agony. And I was like, "Alan, we can just fuckin' move this to another day."

And he's like [*imitates Rickman's British accent*], "You don't have the budget, Kevin; it's a low-budget movie." Even though his back was fucked up big time, he insisted on fuckin' doing the scene. I defy you

to find a moment of pain in that performance. He's just as casual and elegant as he is in everything else. So he loved the movie. Loved hanging out.

He was the guy that jumped up Mewes's performance. 'Cause I kept telling Jason in advance of *Dogma*, I was like, "You can't fuckin' fool around. You gotta memorize the script, man. Not like fuckin' *Mallrats* or *Chasing Amy*. You gotta come correct 'cause we got fuckin' real actors in the movie this time.

And he's like, "What? Like, Affleck?" I was like, "I said real actors, man." He's like, "Like who?" And I said, "We got Alan Rickman in this motherfucker." And he's like, "Who's that?"

And I was like, "Alan Rickman. He's fuckin' Hans Gruber from *Die Hard*, man. 'Yippee-ki-yay, motherfucker.' That guy."

He's like, "Bruce Willis?"

I was like, "The other fuckin' guy."

And he's like, "What about him?"

And I was like, "That dude's fuckin' British, dude. Brits, they invented acting. So if you fuckin' 'snoochie booch' him, he's gonna give you the hard fuckin' stare, man. You gotta be fuckin' on point for this guy. It's a big fuckin' deal. You can't fool around."

Cut to the first rehearsal I do with Jason. We're in Pittsburgh. We're at the hotel, and usually the process of rehearsal begins before everyone else, 'cause it takes a month to teach Jason how to be "Jay". He forgets. So I sat down with him and I was like, "Where's your script?" And he's like, "I don't have it."

And I was like, "How the fuck are we gonna fuckin' rehearse if you don't have your script?"

Alan Rickman, Salma Hayek,
Kevin, and Jason Mewes in
Cannes, 1999

Chris Rock, Ben Affleck, Jason Mewes,
and Matt Damon, 1998

He's like, "I don't need it." And I was like, "You don't need your script?"

He's like, "Try me."

So I was like, "All right." So I open my script, I start reading the scene and he fuckin' did his dialogue. And I was like, "Oh, shit. You memorized that scene."

And he was like, "Try another."

And I flipped through, tried another. He memorized it and I was like, "Jesus Christ! You memorized your scenes. I'm impressed."

He's like, "I did. I memorized all the scenes."

And I was like, "All the scenes you're in?"

He's like, "All the scenes in the movie."

And I was like, "You? Really?"

He goes, "Try me."

I start reading Ben's lines, and he starts saying Matt's lines back to me. Started reading Linda [Fiorentino]'s lines, he started reading [Chris] Rock's lines back to me. And I was like, "Jesus fuckin' Christ! What are you, Rain Man? You memorized the whole fuckin' script, man?"

He's like, "Yeah." I was like, "Why'd you do that?" He's like, "I don't want to piss off that Rickman dude."

So the whole process, I couldn't wait for these two to meet. I met Alan prior to the production and I couldn't wait for him to meet Jason. And it was love at first sight. He hung out with Jason on the movie. This was a big cast, so you're always doing something. You didn't get to hang out as much as you did on other movies. But I would look over periodically off camera, and I would see Jason Mewes and Alan Rickman engaged in conversation. I'd be like, "What the fuck could those two have to say to each other?"

# GOD

**Audience member:** First of all, I really liked *Dogma*.

**Kevin Smith:** Thank you.

**AM:** I was wondering. It's two parts, okay? Do you believe in God?

**KS:** Yes.

**AM:** And why or why not? So, why?

**KS:** Yes, I believe in God. Why? Because I have a career. There can be no better proof for the existence of God than the fact that I have a film career.

Marcus Heath Showalter | Pasco, Washington | "Buddy Christ," 2005

# RECASTING

**Kevin Smith:** Matt [Damon]'s so fuckin' sweet in the movie, and it's so weird because that part wasn't written for him. That part was written for Jason Lee. It was supposed to be Ben playing Bartleby, Jason Lee playing Loki. So when you listen to Loki's dialogue, if you listen really closely, you're like, "Oh, it sounds like Banky [from *Chasing Amy*] and Brodie [from *Mallrats*], 'cause it was meant to be Jason Lee." We were casting the flick and we were still six months out from shooting. We were waiting for a greenlight and Miramax was like, "You gotta get the perfect cast together before we give you more money." So there was this, "We're gonna start now. We're not gonna start." The date was moving all the time.

And Jason Lee was like, "I got an offer to do this movie in France where I speak French and I play a chef, and I think I would like to do that."

I was like, "Okay, but I think we might be shooting *Dogma* in the next six months."

And he's like, "All right. Well, can you confirm that, because I would like to go do this as well?"

And I was like, "But if you do that, man, they might fuckin' not let you be in the movie, 'cause what if we go all of a sudden?"

And he's like, "Well, I wanna do this. So you're not mad, are you?"

I was like, "No, no. Not at all. I totally understand. Go to France. Do the French movie, fuckin' jerk." But I was like, "It's totally fine. It's totally fine." I love Jason, so it didn't matter.

And so, once he was gone, Harvey Weinstein instantly was like, "Oh, Jason Lee's out of the movie. Why don't you get Ben's friend, the famous one, to be in it?"

And thankfully, God bless Matt's heart, he didn't have to. At this point, when we start making this movie, they had already shot *Good Will Hunting*, but it was clear it was going to fuckin' be something. So he could've, at any given moment, been like, "Look, I fuckin' told you back in the day when Jason Lee dropped out that I would do this with you, but I'm a huge fuckin' movie star, so fuck your rinky-dink picture." But he didn't. He stayed with it, and we didn't wind up shooting in that six-month corridor.

When we wound up shooting, Jason Lee was free. He was done with his French movie, so he had called me and he was like, "Hey, man, I'm back. I would love to be in *Dogma* if it's still happening."

And I was like, "I gave your part to Matt Damon." And he was like, "Oh, he's a good actor."

But I was like, "You know what, man? Fuckin' Azrael's still open. You get to play a bad guy."

And he goes, "Oh, I do." And I was like, "Yeah, man. Reread the script." He goes, "I remember. He's kind of like the villain. He explains shit, the plot at the end."

I said, "Yeah, he's our Bond villain."

So he was like, "All right, man. I could get my head around that. Let me do that."

So he wound up doing Azrael, and then, oddly enough, that's the role that kind of led to him being the bad guy in *The Incredibles*. He played Syndrome. He was the voice of the bad guy. And when you watch *Dogma* and fuckin' *The Incredibles* back-to-back, it's almost like he just continued the performance. It's really, really sweet. And he told me that one day. He was like, "Because of *Dogma*, I got the fuckin' Pixar movie."

Jason Lee as Azrael, 1999
*RGR Collection / Alamy Stock Photo*

# REACTION TO THE RELEASE

**Kevin Smith:** When we were getting ready to put it out, it was fucking nuts. We got death threats. We had 300,000 pieces of hate mail and three death threats. Or two. Two and a half death threats. Because I think one recanted toward the end. "I'm gonna fuckin' kill you! Well, maybe not." There was one that I'll never forget and will take it with me to my grave. Not the actual missive, but what it said. I've read it to people so many times that I committed it to memory: "You Jews better take the money you stole from us and buy flak jackets because we're coming in there with shotguns. Your brothers in Christ." The Jews in question were Harvey and Bob Weinstein, who run Miramax and Dimension, who were originally releasing the flick. They got it the worst.

I was Catholic, so people would just be like, "You ought to know better. But your Jew buddies will pay." You don't want to point out that Christ was Jewish because these people tend to forget that. "Jewish? No, he's a WASP." But it was insane. We had to stop receiving mail at the office; they had a service open it. We couldn't receive packages for a year. When we went to Cannes, they wanted to put up metal detectors. The Palais wouldn't let them, so Miramax hired armed bodyguards. It was really a kooky time.

And the whole time, I'm just like, "It's a movie with a fuckin' rubber poop monster in it, you know? Take it easy!" But people judge it, of course, without seeing it. Mostly, the people who were attacking the movie would never see it. They never bothered. If they had watched it, they would've been like, "We'd be stupid to go after it because it's not a threat. There is a rubber poop monster up there on the screen. The kid was right." But they didn't, so we were the way for the group that went after us, the Catholic League, to go after Disney and Miramax, who were the original distributors. They tend to go after Disney quite a bit. If you go after Disney, you get a lot of press. Particularly if you're charging Disney with being anti-Catholic.

The weird thing is, when the Weinsteins bought the movie from Miramax and resold it to Lionsgate, the eventual distributors of the movie, the Catholic League just went away. They made so much noise about "We'll take this movie down. It'll never be seen. It's a true affront to all Catholics. God hates it." When Lionsgate picked it up, [the Catholic League] was like, "We won."

We were like, "How? The movie's still coming out."

# PROTEST

**Kevin Smith:** I read in the *Asbury Park Press* that there was gonna be a protest at our theater in Eatontown, the Sony multiplex. So I said, "Holy shit. I wanna go." I read there was gonna be 1,500 people there. I said, "I'm bound to know some of them because I went to church with them. My mom might be one of them." We got magic markers and glue and sparklies, and we made signs. One of them said, "*Dogma* Is Dogshit." The other one said, "To Hell With *Dogma*." Bryan [Johnson] and I are the youngest people there by about fifty years. We're doing the "Our Father." About fifteen minutes into the fourth decade, a news van pulls up.

I was like, "These people don't know; they'll never know."

A lady gets out, journalist, well-dressed, and she has a clipboard. She comes over. And Bryan's like, "Holy shit." She's looking at her clipboard and looking at me. And she's like, "Are you him?"

I said, "No, no. But I get that all the time."

She was like, "Would you mind if I interviewed you?"

I said, "Please." Because I'm a press whore. So, even if I'm incognito, I'm happy to give an interview.

She's like, "So, what are you doing here tonight?"

I said, "We're protesting this movie."

She said, "Okay. Have you seen it?"

I said, "No, no. But they tell me it's really bad."

She's like, "Have you seen anything else made by the filmmaker?"

I said, "No, no. Well, I saw *Clerks*. That was really funny. But I'm not gonna watch anything else. I'm certainly not gonna watch this."

And she's like, "What's your name?"

And I was like, "Bryan Johnson."

Johnson's like, "We should really go now."

That night on the Channel 12 News, sure enough, "Bryan Johnson" was talking about how bad *Dogma* was. My mother called and was like, "There's somebody on TV looks just like you."

James Kopp (aka Mr. Babes) |
Miami, Florida | "*Dogma*:
Metatron (Alan Rickman),"
2016

# JAY AND SILENT BOB STRIKE BACK

2001

# POLITICS OF DRUGS

SOMETIMES, THE WORLD ON film and the real world bleed into each other. An actor can forget he's playing a role. A filmmaker can forget he's making a movie. For his fifth film, Kevin Smith's characters of Jay and Bob started to blur with the real Jason and Kevin. A movie about two potheads becoming pseudo-celebrities probably felt like a documentary. Truthfully, it took a while for Kevin to become the stoner he wrote about. Jason, on the other hand, had to face the reality that drugs had taken hold of his life, with periods of sobriety and falling off the wagon. Kevin was chasing the dream as Jason was chasing the dragon. While Kevin continued making movies, Jason would eventually get this monkey off his back.

Originally, Jay and Bob were minor roles—just two guys selling weed outside the convenience store. In this film, they became the central characters, and fans loved them as much as, or even more than, Dante and Randal. Except for perhaps Cheech and Chong, Harold and Kumar, or Snoop Dogg, drug culture was not yet in the mainstream. But Kevin's fans, many of whom were casual smokers, could easily relate to these characters and their real-life counterparts. Also, because Jason wasn't pretending to be an addict, the fans were sympathetic and supportive of him, not only in the film but also in the podcast *Jay and Silent Bob Get Old*, where he dealt directly with his drug use and recovery.

# JASON ON DRUGS

**Kevin Smith** [*speaking to actor Jason Mewes*]: At the end of the movie, I opened the trailer door and it was Jekyll and Hyde. You had completely fuckin' changed. Suddenly, you had done oxys or something like that. I came back to see you about thirty days, forty days later to shoot the Afroman video and you had lost twenty to thirty pounds. On me, maybe not even noticeable. On you, it was like looking at a skeleton with skin pulled so tightly over it. And how it happened, it was so strange. I'd pulled up to the house. The door opens and this fuckin' junkie comes out that looked like Mewes. And then that junkie got in my car. I was like, "Oh my God. This ain't no fuckin' junkie. This is Mewes." I remember just bawling and crying. And we had to go shoot a video where we're sitting there pretending to smoke weed with Afroman. And I was like, "I'm going to hell."

Jason Mewes and Tango, the orangutan, 2001
*Courtesy of Tracy Bennett*

# PERSONAL

**Kevin Smith:** It kind of came from a place of—after putting up with a year of the *Dogma* bullshit—just wanting to make a movie that didn't offend anyone or not offend anyone to their spiritual core. If it offended people, it offended people with good taste, just by virtue of the fact that it was a tacky little movie. So it was, in many weird ways, maybe the most personal movie I ever made, even if it's the most ridiculous and broad and very farcical and very pants-droppingest movie we ever made. The humor is certainly not well earned in many places. I always felt like, if you compare it to our other flicks, we earned the laughs by virtue of the fact that what was being said was getting the laughs. Humor through dialogue. This movie was barely that. People falling down and shit like that, real slapsticky.

Used by permission of Media Entertainment, Inc.

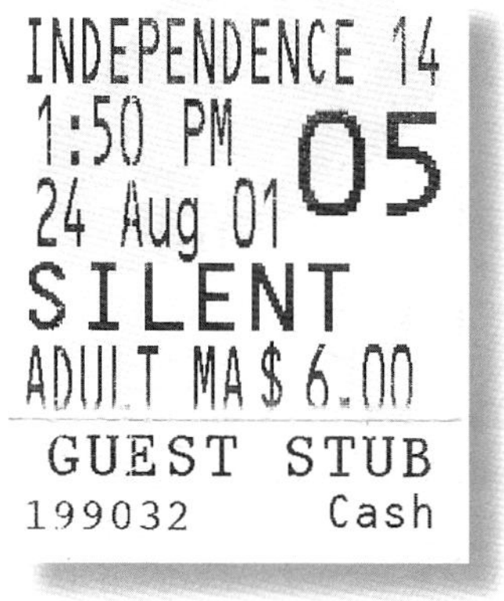

INDEPENDENCE 14
1:50 PM
24 Aug 01  05
SILENT
ADULT MA $ 6.00
GUEST STUB
199032      Cash

"This was the first sneak preview or special screening I ever saw. The date on the ticket matches with the release date though. But I distinctly remember walking through Independence Mall with my Dad, and being surprised that it was listed on the marquee. At this point in time, I owned every single Kevin Smith movie."

—Christopher Kerney

Josué Fuentes | Mérida, Mexico |
"Justice," 2014

Kevin Smith as Silent Bob and Jason Mewes as Jay, 2001
*Entertainment Pictures / Alamy Stock Photo*

# MY BIGGEST FAN

**Kevin Smith:** It's fuckin' nuts that [*Jay and Silent Bob Strike Back*] got made. I remember seeing one person review it online years later and be like, "This is like some fuckin' fan movie. It's like a fan-made movie. It's like some Kevin Smith fan made a movie about Kevin Smith movies."

And I was like, "He did. The world's biggest Kevin Smith fan—Kevin Smith."

Michael Akers | Kingsport, Tennessee | "Kevin Smith," 2015

BLINKY | Los Angeles, California | "Jay and Silent Bob," 2006

# JERSEY GIRL

2004

# IDEALIZED VERSION
# OF AMERICA

**DURING THE RELEASE OF** *Dogma*, Kevin Smith married Jennifer Schwalbach and had their daughter Harley Quinn. So with his sixth film, he decided to explore being a husband and father without inhabiting his movie alter ego. Kevin tried to place himself inside the world of losing his wife and job but still pull from his own experiences. He found a surrogate to help him discover what life might have been like if he'd stayed in Jersey. Since Kevin had always wanted to understand himself through his films, it was really about the life he left behind. The story of a down-on-his-luck PR guy resonated as a way of dealing with a more wholesome version of himself. Now he could inhabit a character who was a family man and who believed the race for money was bullshit.

The casual fan might not have known how important it was for Kevin to set the film in Highlands, New Jersey, where he grew up, nor expected him to do something with such a serious theme. But in this film, he brought his '90s fans into the 2000s, for they were also growing up, getting married, having families, and settling down. Those who knew who Kevin was could see that he was telling this story from a personal place. It took a lot of guts to share and be so vulnerable. And once again, as in *Chasing Amy*, Ben Affleck would be the one taking fans on this cinematic trip.

Kevin with Liv Tyler as Maya and Raquel Castro as Gertie, 2004
*Moviestore Collection Ltd / Alamy Stock Photo*

**KEVIN SMITH**

# BEN AFFLECK

**Kevin Smith:** I started telling [Ben] about this idea for a movie, which would become *Jersey Girl*.

He's like, "I love it. Write it." I said, "I will. When do you wanna do it?" He said, "April." I said, "Yeah. April's good." It was July, and we had a few months. I'd written about thirty, forty pages, and I sent them to him, and he fell in love with it. I told Affleck, "There's a dude checking if you wanna play *Daredevil*."

He's like, "I love *Daredevil*." I said, "That's what I told him." He said, "What'd you say?" I said, "You should play it."

Soon Affleck called me and was like, "I'm doing it. I'm gonna put on the red tights and have the horns." I said, "When do you start?" He goes, "April." I said, "That's when we're doing *Jersey Girl*." He said, "We can wait on *Jersey Girl*. I do *Daredevil*, I get paid my big nut and then we go do *Jersey Girl*, and you pay me fifteen bucks an hour."

I said, "I don't know, man. I think we should do *Jersey Girl* first." He's like, "Don't get upset." I said, "I'm not upset, but fair's fair." He's like, "You recommended me."

"I didn't know it would coincide with *Jersey Girl*. Fuck *Daredevil*." Because I'll turncoat real quickly. I said, "I'm going in April, and if you're there, great. If not, no hard feelings. Go do *Daredevil*. But I want to do something in April. I want to do this movie."

He's like, "Jesus Christ. Look, if you're saying you want me to do *Jersey Girl* in April and you want me to pass on *Daredevil*, I will."

I was like, "Well, if we move the movie to the summer, you have to promise to take far, far less than you normally take." And he was like, "God. Fine, dude. If that'll do it." I said, "Excellent. That means a lot to me."

Then there's a long pause, and he's putting shit together in his mind and he goes, "You didn't finish writing the fucking script yet, did you?"

And I said, "Nope, sucker. Goodbye."

Ben Affleck as Ollie, 2004
AF Archive / Miramax / Alamy Stock Photo

# VILMOS AND RATFACE

**Kevin Smith:** We worked with the DP, Vilmos Zsigmond, the great Vilmos Zsigmond. He won an Academy Award for *Close Encounters of the Third Kind.*

So Ratface . . . that's what [Robert Holtzman] goes by. Ratface was the production designer.

Vilmos on more than one occasion in the movie would be like [*imitates Zsigmond's Hungarian accent*], "Ratface!"

And Ratface would come over like, "Oh my God. He's got an important fuckin' question about the set design." So he'd be like [*imitates Holtzman's Philly accent*], "Yes, Vilmos?"

And Vilmos would be like, "Get me coffee!"

"All right, Vilmos."

Kevin with cinematographer Vilmos Zsigmond, Jennifer Lopez, and Ben Affleck, 2004
*Moviestore Collection Ltd / Alamy Stock Photo*

# CHICAGO TEST SCREENING

**Kevin Smith:** We test screened *Jersey Girl* in Chicago. The last of ten screenings. J.Lo originally made it to the 35-minute mark. In the version we test screened in Chicago, she was dead by the 12-minute mark. And when she died in that Chicago test screening, they played [the song] "Chelsea Dagger" on the loud speakers. That's a hockey joke.

# SNAPSHOT OF HIS LIFE

**Kevin Smith:** It kind of comes from a place of where I am in my life. I've always enjoyed that the movies were snapshots of particular moments in my life. And this one is the kind of snapshot of me as a married guy with a kid, 'cause that's what the movie's about.

Used by permission of Media Entertainment, Inc.

# COMPARING *JERSEY GIRL* TO HIS OTHER FILMS

**Kevin Smith:** Fuck the haters. This movie is cute. *Jersey Girl* is like an adorable niece, whereas *Chasing Amy* is a brainy bi-girl you dream about fucking. *Mallrats* is a bootie-call girl. She doesn't want to date you. You don't want to date her. Whenever you two are bored and alone, it's on. *Clerks* is your first love and the girl who gave you your first blowjob. You will always remember her fondly. *Dogma* is obviously a Catholic schoolgirl, but the kind who does anal. And *Jay and Silent Bob Strike Back* is the dirty fun girl who fucks you in the Denny's bathroom. Next time I have to defend *Jersey Girl*, I'm going to say, "George Carlin loved making it, so go fuck yourself, Mom."

# CASEY AFFLECK'S REVIEW

Casey Affleck wrote an email to Kevin after seeing his brother Ben in the film. Kevin posted this on Instagram: "Casey emailed me the best review of my flick that I'd ever receive." In reference to this email, here's Casey's recollection of that night:

I was invited to see an early test screening of *JERSEY GIRL*. I was surprised by the turn K Smith took with the movie. It was earnest. He had planted a flag in a very different place with his other movies. *JG* was sweet and sincere. It showed a real soft spot. It was the best thing I had seen Ben do. Kevin gave Ben a lot of chances to do different things. This was Ben's best work to date and it was great to see. The whole cast was great. Jennifer Lopez was underused as an actress in her career. I think she has a great screen presence. I wish she had been in more movies. She could now, I guess.

Liv was great. George Carlin, Jason Lee . . . So many of my favorites. The movie is unlike Kevin's work before or after. It is so nice to see other parts of people's personality come out in their work. It's also nice that he never cast me in anything. When I say nice I mean something else. It was a memorable movie night. Everyone in the audience was crying when we left.

—Casey Affleck

# CLERKS II

2006

# OWNING YOUR OWN DESTINY

**RETURNING TO HIS ORIGINAL** inspiration was a way for Kevin Smith to think about being a clerk again. In his seventh film, he revisited this world that he had created, but moved past the basic story by reflecting on his own journey. As in the film, he wanted to burn it down and start over, and it was authentic to what it was while still growing and expanding the characters. Kevin knew that film in general was becoming progressively more like an assembly line. Same old shit repackaged. Referencing our fast-food culture, he could have been accused of the same thing. But he was totally aware of the fact that everything is bought and sold. So he was commenting on society as well as himself.

This film was not only a way to go back to the original, but it also doubled down and gave the fans a nostalgia fix while at the same time updating it. Although many of his younger fans might not have been able to relate to hanging out in a convenience store, they could easily understand chillin' at a McDonald's or, in this case, a Mooby's. Maybe Kevin thought it could be a good way of hooking new fans, just like the way these young kids were already hooked on the burgers and fries.

# ORIGINAL CONCEPT

**Kevin Smith:** There were certain things I knew were going to happen in the movie. It was going to open with the store being on fire. And it was going to be a catalyst to the story. The thing that made them face the future was watching their past burn. I wanted the Talking Heads song "Nothing but Flowers" to open the movie. I knew there was going to be a big dance sequence, and I knew the last shot would pull back from them and go from color to black and white. And I knew at the end of the movie, they would own the Quick Stop. They would be back in the store. The journey would take them from the store to the store. I basically knew the beginning and the end and just needed to fill in everything in between.

# PILLOW PANTS

**Kevin Smith:** We were sitting on the deck at my house, and Jason was sitting there telling me and [Bryan] Johnson about how he's with Jordan [Jason's future wife] but he hasn't made the moves yet. And I said, "That's because she told him that she got a pussy troll."

And Johnson goes, "What?"

And I was like, "It's a troll that lives in her pussy. And she said that if he ever tries to put his dick in her, the troll will bite it off."

And Johnson goes, "Where'd you think of that?"

And I said, "I don't know. But if it existed, it'd be called 'Pillow Pants.'" And he laughed really hard. And years later, I put it in a script just to watch his expression change.

Kevin Smith as Silent Bob and Jason Mewes as Jay, 2006
*United Archives GmbH / Alamy Stock Photo*

# ROSARIO DAWSON

**Scott Mosier:** We were originally like, "No stars. No stars. We don't want any stars." And there was a certain amount of pressure applied by the studio who's financing it to give them a couple names.

**Jon Gordon** [producer]: From a commercial standpoint, I think Harvey [Weinstein] was just trying to show that the movie was not a small little comedy but had the ability to break out beyond that.

**SM:** When you do that, you do a list of names. Everybody writes down a list of names.

**Kevin Smith:** Before he even got to the list, though, he was like [*imitates Harvey Weinstein's New York accent*], "I met with Bryce Dallas Howard." And I was like, "Right on. What was that like?" He was like, "She's a huge fan of yours. We were talking about the movies that we do here, and she brought up *Clerks* and *Chasing Amy*, and she likes your movies." I was like, "That's flattering." He's like, "So you should meet with her. She's who you should talk to about *Clerks II.*"

So I sit down with her and I brought a copy of the *Clerks II* script with me and I gave it to her and I was like, "Right on, man. Let me know what you think?" And she read it, and I guess it might have been a little too bracing for her.

**SM:** And she passed on it. So next we went to Ellen Pompeo, who at that point had *Grey's Anatomy* in the can, and they were waiting for it to come out. So we went out to her.

**KS:** I'd seen her in some episodes of *Law & Order*. I'm a huge *Law & Order* fan. I really liked her and I really liked her look and she seemed believable, like maybe she would fuck Dante.

**SM:** And she seemed interested, but I think everyone was getting the suspicion that the show would take off, and I don't know exactly what happened, but she ended up moving on.

**JG:** There was a conversation about Liv [Tyler]. Actually, Kevin talked to Liv about it. And Liv had just had a baby and she said, "I can't say things like, 'Ass to mouth.'" And she had a three-week old at home.

**SM:** So then there became a list of people. There was a list of five or six people, and one of them was Sarah Silverman.

**KS:** And she was like, "If you were offering me the part of Randal, I would do it in a heartbeat 'cause that's the fuckin' part." She's going, "But I just don't want to play the girl in the movie now. I'm trying to go in a different direction." And I was like, "I got it."

**SM:** There was a list, and Rosario Dawson was on it. And Rachel Weisz.

**JG:** Yeah. There was Rachel Weisz. That was never happening.

**KS:** We were like, "Rosario Dawson ain't gonna do this fuckin' picture. Not in a fuckin' million years, man."

**SM:** There's no fuckin' way she's going to do it.

**JG:** 'Cause Rosario does classy pictures. She doesn't do *Passion of the Clerks* [the original title].

**Rosario Dawson:** My manager and my agent went into the office and read the script. So they brought it over and they were like, "You have three hours."

**SM:** When the script got to her, I was like, "How quickly will she decide not to do it?"

**JG:** You never know how anyone is going to react, especially when you are a name actress and you get a script and you read it and you think, "Okay, who are the actors I'm going to be acting opposite in this movie?" And it's two actors who nobody knows, you may be a little hesitant to do that movie.

**RD:** I was reading along and going, "This is really good. It's really well written." But when the donkey show came in, I was like, "This is my opportunity to see a donkey show. This is a yes. This is a no-brainer. This is amazing."

**SM:** She fuckin' said she wanted to do it, which is great, but I thought there was no chance in hell.

**KS:** I really felt like Rosario was so much better than Bryce, and not like they're not good actresses, but just, in terms of the character of Becky, made more sense than Bryce, than Ellen, than Sarah. She's a New Yorker, and she had this East Coast feel to her that I felt would blend really well with Becky.

Trevor Fehrman as Elias, Brian O'Halloran as Dante, Rosario Dawson as Becky, and Jeff Anderson as Randal, 2006
*United Archives GmbH / Alamy Stock Photo*

# DOUBTS

**Kevin Smith:** The night before we started shooting, I was down in Buena Park in my motel room. And I'd set up my TV and my DVD player and I actually, for the first time in eons, watched *Clerks*. And I went back to the place where I made the movie, in terms of where I was in my head and in my heart. And I was like, "No. I'm in the exact right place where I need to be in order to make *Clerks II*. This is a totally good idea. This movie honors the first movie and it doesn't try to be better than it, or worse than it, or even equal to it. But it just tries to be its own fuckin' movie that happens to carry those characters and the scenario over a little bit."

Carla Rodrigues | Porto, Portugal |
"Dante & Randal," 2006

# SOBER JASON

**Jason Mewes** [as Jay in *Clerks II*]: We got six months and two days on the wagon as a good friend of Bill W's [founder of Alcoholics Anonymous].

**Kevin Smith:** We were talking about this last night. This is the first movie that you've made completely fuckin' SLP, sober living pal, 'cause on *Clerks* . . .

**JM:** Drinking and smoking weed.

**KS:** *Mallrats*?

**JM:** Just drinking. Oh, drinking and smoking weed a little bit.

**KS:** *Chasing Amy*?

**JM:** I was on dope. *Dogma*. Coke and dope.

**KS:** *Jizzle and Bizzle*? [*Jay and Silent Bob Strike Back*]

**JM:** Drinking. And the last week, I was on painkillers.

**KS:** *Jersey Girl*?

**JM:** I wasn't there.

**KS:** Because?

**JM:** I was on drugs. Running from the law. That was at the very time I was running from the cops, even.

Nicholas Chamberlain | Seattle, Washington | "Jay and Silent Bob," 2017

# QUENTIN TARANTINO

**Kevin Smith** [*speaking to director Quentin Tarantino*]: When I started writing [*Clerks II*], I remember a conversation that we had had back at Munich in '94. We were talking about *Clerks* and you were like, "I dig it, but it's not really a movie, is it?" You said, "It's just really a series of stand-up comedy set in a movie format." I was like, "Yeah. It was very joke oriented." And this one, for me, was more like, there are jokes, but there's an arc, you know.

**Quentin Tarantino:** Oh no, no, no. Very much so. And by the way, what I said before, that wasn't an insult.

**KS:** I never took it as a criticism. It's true, and to just do the same thing again would have been like, "Why bother?" Doing a sequel is always negligible, but this never felt like a sequel to me as much as a continuation. And one that I couldn't have done in '95 because there was just not enough life experience. It would have been the same movie then; whereas now, that movie was kind of like what it was like for me to be twenty, and this movie is kind of what it's like to be thirty.

Kevin, Quentin Tarantino, and Bryan Johnson
at the Munich Film Festival, 1994

# CANNES

*This was recorded outside the Palais at the Cannes Film Festival before the premiere of* Clerks II *on May 26, 2006.*

**Kevin Smith:** Here we are in Cannes, the morning of our premiere. This behind us is the theater where we'll be screening. It's the Debussy. It's the other theater in the Palais. Something bad's bound to happen. You know, maybe the reviews come out and it's like [*imitates French accent*], "This is shit." The Catholic in me is waiting for punishment.

**KS** [*after the Cannes screening*]: In the midst of the screening I was like, "This is playing better than *Clerks* played when we were here or *Dogma* played when we were here. I mean, this is a fantastic fuckin' screening." People were dialed in. They were laughing in all the right places. Standing ovation begins. And once they stood and started applauding, I was like, "That's fuckin' awesome." Once it kept going on and on and finally hit the eight-minute mark, I was like, "This is the best experience I've ever had at this film festival."

*Clerks II* premiere, walking on the red carpet
at the Cannes Film Festival (Rosario Dawson,
Kevin, Jennifer Schwalbach, Scott Mosier,
and Jeff Anderson), 2006

*Clerks II* InAction Figures, 2006
*Courtesy of Graphitti Designs*

Scott Finnis | New York | *"Clerks 2 –
Randal Graves – Clerks TAS [The Animated
Series]* style," 2014

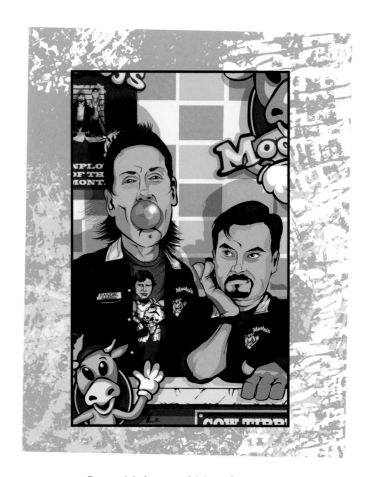

Peter Mahoney | Manchester,
United Kingdom | "Funployees,"
2007

**KEVIN SMITH**

Katie Atkins | Auckland, New Zealand | "Jay and Silent Bob," 2014

# ZACK AND MIRI MAKE A PORNO

2008

# SEX EDUCATION

**FOR HIS EIGHTH FILM.** Kevin Smith tackled the seedy world of pornography. But the subject never offended him or his attitude about sex. Believing that society had finally caught up with him, he realized this was a story that best suited his sensibilities. By combining sweetness with hardcore content, he had reached a new comedic level, which would give him the confidence to take on even greater challenges.

Kevin wanted to do a romantic comedy his way, and the fans were cool with that. Maybe doing something traditional was out of his comfort zone. He has a real gift for delving into controversial subjects, such as religion, drugs, or pornography, and flipping them. His fans loved seeing his take on this topic—not by marginalizing it, but by making light of it . . . mocking, parodying pop culture, and dismantling it.

# ZACK AND MIRI MAKE A PORNO REVIEW [EXCERPT]

## BY BRIAN PRISCO, OCTOBER 10, 2008
### COURTESY OF PAJIBA.COM

Kevin Smith made a movie, y'all. An honest to god, motherfucking movie. For years, people have been busting out slacker comedies with chubby stoners finding inexplicably hot girlfriends or basic romantic comedies sprinkled with a couple dick and fart jokes. They have never paid respect to the man who, while not the father of the genre (Richard Linklater), is assuredly the son if not the holy fucking spirit. The difference is they would triple the budget, slap in a couple of hot-in-the-moment comedians, pull back on the f-bombs, and rake in mad amounts of cash. Kevin Smith sat back, let the boys play, while he went about his business making a couple of movies with his friends. Then came *Zack and Miri Make a Porno*. It's a little like Pete Wentz jamming in front of a couple of sorority girls, impressing them with all three of the chords he knows. When Tom Morello walks in, Pete says, "Hey, Tom, how you like my new guitar?" Tom picks it up and says, "Boy, let me tell you what." He then busts out a riff that makes all of the girls wearing panties wet them, spontaneously impregnate, and orgasms all the girls in the coffee shop next door. And then he smiles, hands back the guitar, and walks away, as Wentz's mascara runs down his face.

Congratulations everyone else making dick and fart joke romantic comedies. You just got fucking served.

Zack (Seth Rogen), a barista at a knock-off chain, lives with his best friend Miri (Elizabeth Banks) who might have a job? When it looks like they're going to lose their home, they decide to make a porno movie hoping to earn a shitload of money fast.

It's the thinnest of plots, and if you saw it on a DVD cover, you'd laugh and throw it back in the $5 bin next to *Wargames: The Dead Code* and the *Olsen Twins Double Trouble Feature Pack*.

But in a Kevin Smith movie, you don't worry about the blueprints so much as how the finished home feels. Most of his films have the barest inkling of a plot, while careening along on the charm and witticisms of the cast. And it works. You don't watch for the cinematography. You listen for the killer rapport between the real folks. This movie assuredly does not disappoint. Smith turns on all four cylinders with pop culture riffs, vulgarity, witty exchanges, and even more slurs. Unlike most movies of this ilk, where moviegoers will regurgitate only the pre-packaged comedy bits (you know how I know you're gay?), *Zack and Miri* bursts with constant gems. It doesn't matter the scene. I can't give you any snippets without completely ruining surprises. Well, alright, let's just say the title of the proposed porno goes from *Star Whores: The Phantom Man-Ass* to something involving the phrase "cockachino." You'll never think of a frosted cupcake the same way again. Like a Mifune samurai, Smith has honed his craft to almost effortless killing capacity. It's why people love *It's Always Sunny in Philadelphia*: because the characters are absolute bastards to one another because they genuinely care about everyone. This is particularly evident in the use of racial humor. In *Clerks II*, we started out with Hooper X and then moved on to the porch monkey chatter. They felt a little slapped in for shock value. Here, he's managed to weave it in with the rest of the banter to create brilliance. When a customer interrupts the black barista to request a "Coffee. Black." Delaney says, "We're talking here. White."

Smith is smart enough to let Zack and Miri's relationship be the main focus of the movie and not get wrapped up in throwing in as many cock-and-balls chuckles as he can. He has finally found the perfect balance of raunch and romance, and it blends so smoothly you sometimes forget the movie is about fucking. It's downright profane, it's crass, it's crude, but it's also quite endearing. Towards the end, Smith gets practically Capraesque with his sentimentality, but he's also careful to deflate any moment that seems a little too precious. Heartfelt confessions of love are exchanged while people are on the toilet, without making it some sort of fart joke. While he avoids the complex, difficult ending of *Chasing Amy*, the ending of *Zack and Miri* is still incredibly satisfying without being sappy.

Indeed, the movie leaves you feeling almost buoyant. What makes it work so well is that you can see in every frame the cast is having a fucking ball. The sheer joy of making this movie resonates in every scene. The supporting cast is particularly splendid, a veritable hodgepodge of View Askew regulars, comedians, and porn stars. Jeff Anderson pulls off a less snarky Randall [*sic*] for this, but it fully works for the character. Lester is Jason Mewes' finest performance because he's not relying on snoochie boochies for a laugh. He's still absolutely fucking off the wall, doing completely crazy shit, but he's actually acting for a change. Ricky Mabe, a big star in Canada, is going to get recognition for this. It's not quite as breakout as Elias from *Clerks II*, but Mabe makes the most of his small part. Craig Robinson finally gets a meatier role as Delaney, Zack's co-worker at the coffeehouse. He practically steals every scene he's in. If you've never seen Traci Lords or Katie Morgan naked, you probably don't own a computer and still refer to flushable commodes as "terlets." Neither of them take themselves seriously, so they're able to just have fun with their respective parts, and it works surprisingly well. In fact, Katie Morgan was giving me a Joey Lauren Adams vibe, only filled with silicone. Speaking of naked, and I know everyone's wondering: You do see Seth Rogen's ass, but no Elizabeth Banks nudity. Don't fret, gents, because there's more than enough inflatable boobies to save the entire cast of *Tit-tanic*. And ladies, if Rogen ain't doing it for you, I offer an uncomfortably full-frontal Jason Mewes. So uncomfortably naked.

*Shudder*

Elizabeth Banks as Miri and Seth Rogen as Zack, 2008
*AF Archive / The Weinstein Company / Alamy Stock Photo*

# SETH ROGEN

**Kevin Smith:** I had this transparent blotter on my desk. And so the whole time I'm writing *Zack and Miri*, it says, "Seth Rogen," with his phone number under it. And when I was done with the script, I was like, "I can't call this dude. It's going to seem so fuckin' weird if I'm just calling this dude who I met barely once for like two minutes in a hotel."

**Scott Mosier:** And between that meeting and us approaching him to do the movie, *Knocked Up* came out. *Superbad* came out while we approached him. All that stuff happened.

**KS:** So I'd sent him an email and I said, "You may not remember me. We met very briefly for about two minutes about a year and a half ago, something like that. But I've been writing this script called *Zack and Miri Make a Porno* with you in mind as the lead. I wrote it for you."

**Seth Rogen:** I might have heard rumblings before that. I heard that Kevin might be writing something with you in mind. You hear that, not a lot, but you hear something like that and it's never true.

**KS:** So I sent it. Less than four minutes later, "You've got mail." And it was a response from Rogen and he said, "No bullshit. When I first came out to Los Angeles, I sat down with an agent who said, 'What do you want to do?'"

**SR:** And I said, "One of my goals was to be in a Kevin Smith movie."

**KS:** Fuckin' score. The dude's a fan.

**SR:** And I guess I didn't know that Kevin Smith movies weren't that financially successful, 'cause when you're young, that kind of doesn't make as much difference. And I remember one of them said, "That's probably easier than you think."

# ELIZABETH BANKS

**Kevin Smith:** [Seth] immediately sparked to Elizabeth Banks. He was like, "Banks, she was in [*40-Year Old*] *Virgin*. And she got close for *Knocked Up*."

**Elizabeth Banks:** I got a call that there was a short list, and maybe I was on it. And maybe I could go and sit down at Kevin's house.

**KS:** So Banks came here to read it. She went in the living room. An hour and a half later, we sat out at the deck of the house, just bullshitting for about an hour.

**EB:** Kevin, when he was pitching me on Miri, said that he felt that the reunion scene was Miri's comedy peak in the movie, which happens in the first fifteen minutes. So I just thought, "Dude, I gotta be funny for another hour, so we're going to need to find some more peaks and valleys."

# SHIT SHOT

**Elizabeth Banks:** There's a moment in the movie that, when I first read the movie, I thought, "Well, this is just too much. This is the one moment in the movie that is over the top. This will never get through. This will never be in the movie." And frankly, it makes me a little uncomfortable. It makes me sick even thinking about this moment in the movie. And that, of course, is the moment when Jeff gets shat on.

**Kevin Smith:** So the shit shot in the flick starts on the page, of course. It's a concept in the script.

**Jeff Anderson:** I knew I was this Deacon character, and I was kind of reading through the script and going through it, and I thought the script was funny. I was excited for my character because he's in a lot of scenes, doesn't have a lot of dialogue; so immediately I was feeling nice and relaxed and relieved. And somewhere through the script, I'm reading along and I'm looking at it and I'm like, "Ha, ha, ha, this poor sap gets shit on. This is great." Then I was like, "Wait a minute. Deacon. That's me!"

# SHOOTING SEX

**Kevin Smith:** The sex shit was nerve-racking, initially. You just never want to get into that moment with somebody where you're like, "Okay, so you're going to need to take your blouse off now." It's just a weird feeling to ask somebody to get naked unless you're going to try to put your dick in 'em.

You could not have asked for two more perfect people [Jason Mewes and Katie Morgan] to A, have that conversation; B, shoot that scene; C, shoot it multiple times. Because you have one guy who doesn't mind being naked. He has been air-fucking his whole life. And you have one lady who—that's what she does. She's done a lot of filmed fucking.

# TRIMMING DOWN

**Scott Mosier:** So we leave Pittsburgh and we get back to L.A. Kevin was cutting along the way, like he always does. And he had a lot of the movie already cut together by the time we got back to L.A., [so] we submitted that to the MPAA [Motion Picture Association of America]. That cut got an NC-17.

**Kevin Smith:** And they said, "Look. You know, a lot of it is adult material, wall to wall. But you might want to look very closely at all the thrusting in the Lester and Stacey porno sequence. There's way too much thrusting. The other area was the shit shot."

# MPAA

**Kevin Smith:** Of all the movies that are made, only 4 percent ever bother to try the MPAA appeals process. Most just cut until they get the rating. Of the 4 percent that try the appeals process, less than 1 percent have successfully flipped the rating. So I've done it twice before [on *Clerks* and *Jersey Girl*] and I'm praying to God I'm going to do it for my third time, but I'm not feeling it. I'm like, "I don't think I'm going to get this." So I'm nervous about flipping. I'm on the verge of saying to Joan [Graves, head of the Classification and Rating Administration], "Let's cut a deal." If this is like fuckin' *Law & Order*, let's cut a deal. That's what they do on that show. I'm thinking like, "I'll drop all the thrusting you want me to drop, but you gotta give me the shit shot. I need that shit shot. Please don't take the shit shot away from me." Trying to make a deal before the verdict comes in. And I'm just about to say it to Joan. I'm just about to say, "Joan . . ." and all of a sudden, boom! The screening-room door opens, and the woman comes out and she says, "They overturned it. It's an R-rated film."

# PARENTING TIPS

**Kevin Smith** [*speaking to producer Scott Mosier*]: [In] the *Boston Herald* this week, there was a piece about some children studies teacher objecting to the posters and insisting they be pulled down from public spaces . . .

**Scott Mosier:** Because of the word "porno"?

**KS:** Because of the word "porno" and also she cited the stick figure drawings as well because she's like, "That's going to draw a child's eye." It's going to draw a child's eye to it because it's a very basic drawing or cartoon so children are going to look at it and, if they're reading age, they're going to be like, "What's porno?"

**SM:** Here's the plan. Say no. Don't take your five-year-old to the movie.

**KS:** I was talking to Jen [Kevin's wife] two weeks ago about the schedule coming up, and I was like, "Then I'm going to go here. And then there's a *Zack and Miri* this, and I saw a *Zack and Miri* poster outside." And the kid was sitting at Jen's desk doing homework. She was in the room, but around her we've never said *Zack and Miri Make a Porno*. All through production, Jen was like, "Just call it *Zack and Miri*." So I was saying "*Zack and Miri*" and then there was a lull in our conversation. And quietly from the desk, I heard, "*Make a Porno.*"

And I was like, "What? What did you say?" And she's like, "It's called *Zack and Miri Make a Porno*, right?" And I was like, "It is. Do you know what porno is? And she goes, "That's what you do for a living." And I was like, "All right." She's wrong, but she has a vague idea . . .

**SM:** That it's a form of a movie.

**KS:** That it's a form of entertainment or a movie that is not for her, 'cause she knows that what I do for a living is make movies for grown-ups. So at that point I said, "Yes and no. Dad's never made a porno, although

this movie is called it. But it's not really. But a porno is just a grown-up movie that you won't see for years and years." And that was it. There were no further questions. There was no, like, "What do you mean? Why can't I see it? I want to see it now." She had no interest because there's no draw for a child. You know what I'm saying? What parent is afraid of just simply saying to their kid, "A porno is a grown-up movie that you can't see."

Kevin and Harley on the set of *Zack and Miri Make a Porno*

# COP OUT

2010

# CELEBRITY

**FOR HIS NINTH FILM,** it's ironic that Kevin Smith achieved his goal of working with Bruce Willis and then thought about abandoning the film industry and retiring from directing altogether. He wanted to blow everything up, and it was this experience that turned him back to his independent roots. Kevin reached a point where achieving a certain box-office number was not satisfying anymore, that profitability had  lost its purpose. It was never why he wanted to be a filmmaker. It was now time to decide whether he could become a studio hack or leave the shit behind and do it on his own.

Kevin had been a big fan of Bruce Willis and liked the idea that they had something in common: both were from New Jersey. He took on a huge Hollywood movie with one of the biggest stars in the world and was excited about directing his favorite actor. But as it turned out, Bruce didn't want to go along with Kevin being the puppet master who sometimes treated his actors like ventriloquist dummies. Even though the majority of critics weren't with him, he knew the fans would be.

THE FOLLOWING WAS POSTED ON FEBRUARY 27, 2010, BY NICK SALYERS ON HIS WORDPRESS BLOG AND IS REPRINTED HERE IN ITS ENTIRETY.

# COP OUT REVIEW

This review contains no spoilers. Read with no risk. *Cop Out* is the touching story of two detectives that must overcome their differences in order to stop a notorious drug dealer from expanding his empire. Oh yeah, and Bruce Willis and Tracy Morgan are in it, and they fuck up the other guys' investigation. I kid, I kid, but in reality, the movie is funny. Rather than being your typical buddy cop movie, where two unlikely partners are paired up within the first five minutes and have to bond, the movie opens with their nine-year partnership anniversary, and, though they fight throughout the movie, you realize that they truly like each other, and act accordingly several times.

Personally, Anna and I loved it. The action was pretty good, the movie had good pacing and never really felt boring, and, unsurprisingly, the movie was funny. As hell. There were maybe three or four times I ever stopped laughing throughout the movie. It was uproarious. Many of the jokes I was able to predict the punchline, ending, or twist, but in each case this wasn't a disappointment. It was just a confirmation of what I found hilarious. What's that? You want a simple way to know if you're going to like *Cop Out*? Well, you're in luck, there's a good, simple way of figuring out whether you're going to like this movie or not. Really easy. I mean ridiculously easy. Okay, here it goes. Name the movie that this quote comes from. "Say, would you like a chocolate covered pretzel?" If you said *Toy Story*, congratulations, you're a dumbass. If, however, you said *Mallrats*, then congratulations, you're going to like *Cop Out*. Now, I know this isn't the best litmus test. You can like *Mallrats* and possibly hate *Cop Out*, and you can like *Cop Out* without having seen *Mallrats*, but I'm here to tell you that you will be the exception. "But Nick," you say. "I want a number score!" Well, fuck you. And fuck the critics who both feel the need to rate according to a number or letter grade and do so poorly. Fuck you so much that I'm going to give my numerical rating in fuck-yous. *Cop Out* gets 5 Fuck Yous out of 5. Go see this movie.

KEVIN SMITH

# TRACY MORGAN

**Kevin Smith** [*speaking to comedian Jay Mohr*]: [Tracy] saved our asses. He made like nineteen movies while we were trying to make just the one.

**Jennifer Schwalbach:** He powered through. He was having some health problems . . .

**KS:** He had his kidney replaced within the last calendar year. We're making *Cop Out*. He's got diabetes, right? Diabetics, they've got to look out for their feet big-time. He's got a hole in his foot and he has to wear this device. He's got this boot he's got to wear. You put it on. It's got a tube that goes into the hole, and it's got a tube that goes to a unit that he's got to carry that runs and suctions out the moisture to promote healing. So this dude is literally fuckin' acting with this fuckin' contraption. This dude's fuckin' doing as funny as he can, nineteen different fuckin' movies, shows up on time . . .

**Jay Mohr:** And that's rare for a person of Tracy's color . . . [*shocked laughter erupts*]. No. You guys totally misunderstood what I said.

Tracy Morgan as Paul, 2010
*AF Archive / Warner Bros. / Alamy Stock Photo*

# TRACY AD-LIBS WITH BRUCE

**Kevin Smith:** Tracy had just watched *Frankenstein* the night before. And before we shot the scene, he was standing next to me. He was like [*imitates Tracy Morgan*], "Kev! D'you ever see *Frankenstein*? I just watched it last night." And then he starts doing lines from *Frankenstein*. "You know his assistant's name is fuckin' Fritz. He never treated Fritz right." And I realize, "Tracy, you're working bits on me. You're testing out material. I get it. That's hysterical."

All of a sudden, we're shooting this take. Bruce is not doing the script, and Tracy has a look of like, "Well, fuck this. The gloves are off." He takes a sip of his fuckin' drink and he goes, "Jimmy, d'you ever see *Frankenstein*?" And I was sitting behind the monitor going, "I bet you he's going to do that whole fuckin' bit." And sure enough, he did the entire run that he had just done for me, but even fuckin' longer. Acting out lines.

Bruce Willis . . . I could see him on the monitor. You watch his face go from puzzlement to fear to intolerance. At first he was like, "What the fuck is he talking about? Are these the scripted lines?" He's trying to remember the fuckin' script. And then all of a sudden he's terrified because he's like, "I don't know where I am or what I'm supposed to do and this guy is talking about fuckin' *Frankenstein*. Did I get the right script for this movie?"

And then finally intolerance. He just stopped acting and looked at Tracy in disbelief with this expression of, like, "If you're going to do this all by yourself, I'm just going to sit here and fuckin' watch." And finally the take ended, and I was like, "Cut!" And everyone was applauding 'cause Tracy was fuckin' brilliant. And the only guy in the room who was not applauding, but he had a smile on his face, was Bruce. He just had this calm smile on his face.

There's a picture of us, me and Bruce, behind the monitor on this day, and it's on IMDb. I've seen it online. And I realized it's the moment I lost him.

**KEVIN SMITH**

Bruce Willis and Kevin at the monitor, 2010
*AF Archive / Warner Bros. / Alamy Stock Photo*

# DAVID ADDISON

**Kevin Smith:** Tracy's admitting something and Bruce's character has got to be there for it. We do it, and he's totally good in it, but I'm looking for something very specific. So I do another take. I'm like, "That's good. Let's go one more." We do another take and it's still not emerging naturally. I'm praying that it'll just accidentally happen, so I don't have to go fuckin' talk to him. The AD [assistant director] goes, "We're good? We moving on? Wanna check the gate?" I go, "Ah, you know what? Check it." I sit there for twenty seconds thinking. I nut up and I'm like, "You know what? Hold on. We're gonna go one more. Gimme a sec."

I go over to Bruce and I'm like, "Hey, boss. Um . . . I don't know how to say this, man, so I'm just going to come out and say it. I was looking for something very specific, and I know this is going to go over like a lead balloon, but I'm just going to say it or else I'm going to hate myself for not saying it. What I'm looking for is this look that David Addison gave Maddie in the second season [of the TV show *Moonlighting*]. It was in the episode where Maddie thinks her father is cheating on her mother. Maybe it was called 'I Am Curious . . . Maddie.' It had 'Papa Was a Rollin' Stone' running throughout."

Now he was looking at me, and he goes, "Wait a second, Kevin. Did you just ask me to give a performance that I gave twenty-five years ago?"

Then I was like, "No?"

And he's like, "No! Goddammit. You know what, Kevin? Go back to the monitor."

I was like, "All right. My bad. I'm sorry. All right, everybody. One more. We're going one more." I sit behind the monitor. I just wait and see what happens, 'cause I figure he's going to give the same fuckin' performance he always does. I say "Action!" Goddamn, two lines in, David Addison shows up. It was spellbinding.

And then he's walking by after the take and he goes, "That was for you, Kev."

Bruce Willis is an international star. Here he is on a poster in Sajóvámos, a Hungarian village, selling the energy drink Hell, 2018.
*Courtesy of Sally Gati*

Rick Fortson (aka Dr. Pencil) |
Oswego, Illinois | "Bruce Willis," 2010

# RED STATE

2011

# FANATICISM

**MAKING HIS TENTH FILM** about violent and immoral religious fanatics seemed to be quite a departure for Kevin Smith. He no longer wanted to be viewed as only a comedy director, and he never really saw himself as defined by his previous films. His goal of reinvention had begun. Taking cues from Quentin Tarantino, he felt that he could tell a badass story but retain his signature style. Breaking away from his past films, instead of using jokes as his weapon of choice, he used guns.

Kevin realized he didn't need to have superstars in his films because, for his fans, the director was the star. He decided to do a traveling roadshow and tour the movie around the country, with Q&As where he got to talk directly to his fans. This was a big part of the movie's marketing. And when he showed the film at Sundance, he said he'd forgo releasing it through a studio because he knew he'd have fan support if he released it himself.

# FRED PHELPS

**Kevin Smith** [*speaking with documentary filmmaker Malcolm Ingram*]: Without Malcolm, *Red State* probably wouldn't exist. It was seeing Malcolm's interview footage with Fred Phelps [pastor at the Westboro Baptist Church] on his documentary *Small Town Gay Bar* that made me go, "Oh my God. This guy could be an awesome movie villain, an over-the-top fundamentalist preacher."

Michael Parks as Pastor Abin Cooper and John Goodman as ATF Agent Joseph Keenan, 2011
*RGR Collection / Alamy Stock Photo*

# SAM JACKSON

**Kevin Smith** [*speaking to casting director Deborah Aquila*]: Early on in this movie, we wanted to put John Goodman in it. It was one of the first names that came up for this role of Keenan in the movie. Problem was, when we were planning on shooting, he was still working on *Treme*, so he was unavailable. He was N/A, not available, on the sheet. And I was like, "Fuck!" So we started going around like, "Who else would be cool?" So I had gone to the San Diego Comic-Con, and I was waiting to go do a Q&A that I do there every year. And upstairs at Comic-Con, there was a bunch of the Marvel movie people.

So who's up there but fuckin' Sam Jackson. He's like, "Kev!"

And I was like, "Hey, man. How are you?"

And he's like, "Nothing, man. Just doing this Marvel thing. What are you doing?"

I said, "We're getting ready to shoot a movie, hopefully in the fall. This little movie. Way beneath the stuff that you guys do."

He's like, "You got something in there for me?"

"If you're interested, yeah. I'll see about sending you a script."

And so we went out to Sam Jackson. I was like, "We don't have any cash."

[Producer] Jon Gordon was like, "What's our move? We can't offer him anything but fuckin' scale. We're doing a favored nations kind of thing."

And I said, "Well, I know Sam Jackson's into graphics. I have these two awesome Gottfried Helnwein paintings. They're worth probably close to a couple million bucks. They've appreciated over the years from when I bought them. One gigantic dark Mickey Mouse painting.

And one that's two LAPD cops from circa 1950, but they're standing over the body of a fallen Donald Duck." So I said, "You know what, man? Let's offer Sam these paintings. I know it's kind of unorthodox, but let's go wampum style. I will trade you goods for services."

So we called back his agent, who's being a real hardnose, like, "You gotta come back to us with a money offer. This is bullshit."

And we came back and said, "All right. Here's a money offer. There will be no money. But we're going to give you two paintings that are worth close to two million dollars."

"Well, I can't go back to Sam with that. We can't take Kevin's artwork off of his wall."

So I was so steamy about it, and I called you and you were like, "Please leave me out of this. I know you pick fights with everybody, Kevin, but I don't want to be a part of this jihad."

I was like, "We're going to burn it all down, Deb. It's all coming down."

But she was like, "Let's concentrate on the matter at hand. Don't take your eye off the ball. Instead of worrying about fuckin' who you need to get revenge on, let's fill this role."

And I was like, "Okay."

And you were like, "I've got very good news for you."

I was like, "What?"

And you were like, "John Goodman's available and our dates finally lined up. He's done with *Treme*."

Gottfried Helnwein, *Midnight Mickey*, 2001. Oil and acrylic on canvas, 216 x 300 cm
*Courtesy of Studio Helnwein*

**KEVIN SMITH**

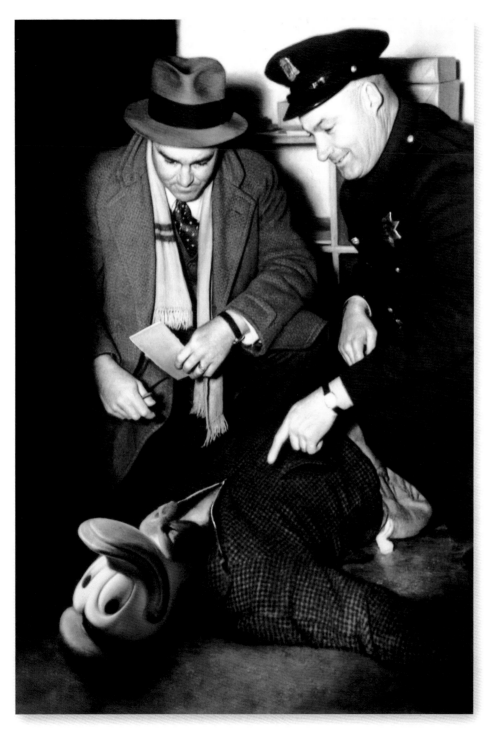

Gottfried Helnwein, *L.A. Confidential (Cops II)*, 2000. Oil and acrylic on canvas, 70 x 48 in (178 x 122 cm) *Courtesy of Studio Helnwein*

# SUNDANCE PROTEST

**Audience member:** I've seen you spar with the actual Phelpses on Twitter. And they're kind of intertwined with this film a lot. What was the protest like at Sundance?

**Kevin Smith:** There was this little snow hill, and they were standing on top of it with two signs apiece, maybe one hung up behind their head as well. And they just looked like hateful scarecrows from the old *Planet of the Apes*. It forced you to be creative in a dopey way, because their signs are so fuckin' dumb that you just try to come up with equally dumb signs. And the one that Jon Gordon had said, "I'm a Happy Jew." And on the back, it had a smiley face with a yarmulke cut into the top and a Star of David. In case they couldn't read English, you could flip around to the pictograph. And then Malcolm's sign said, "Dick Tastes Yummy." And I liked that that was held up next to the Phelpses.

It was so nice listening to the kids' counterprotest. It warmed my heart. "Oh, nice. We can always count on youth to fuckin' fight idiocy or fuckin' intolerance." But the whole thing lasted—I thought it was a half an hour.

Somebody told me today, "You were out there for six minutes."

I was like, "That's it? Wow! Felt a lot longer."

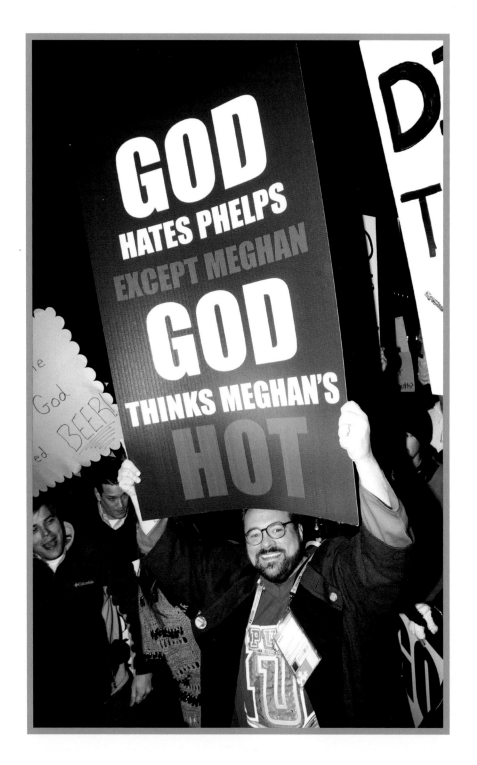

Kevin counter-protesting at the
Sundance screening of *Red State*, 2011
*AP Photo / Danny Moloshok*

**KEVIN SMITH**

# CUTTING THE SUNDANCE CUT

**Kevin Smith:** Yesterday, me and Jon Gordon sat down with the movie and took time out. I want to say we took seven minutes out. As you've seen from the last piece, there's that six-minute, seven-minute clip of Michael Parks as we roll credits. I love that performance. We're going to keep a majority of it, but the problem is, we never saw it play in front of a real audience. At the screening in our house at the end of the movie when it wrapped, we showed the movie, we had credits. You have a house full of people who worked on the movie. Guess what each credit brought up, "Whooo!"

So at Sundance, same kind of thing happened. First credit comes up over picture. Everyone's like, "Whooo!" Movie's over. But we get six more minutes of this motherfucker muttering to himself in a cell. So it's just like, "Oh shit." In that way, we have to go a bit more traditional, inasmuch as we have to give the movie a finite ending and cut to black and start our credits and let a song play. There's a sense of, "Is it done? Is it not done? Wait, it's done. Oh, he's laying down. Oh no, he's not done. He's getting up."

And Bob Weinstein, after he saw the movie, he was like [*imitates Weinstein*], "If you love your actor, you'll cut that end scene a little bit." And I was like, "Why?"

He was like, "It's just too much. I don't care if you're Laurence Olivier. If I'm looking at you that much, I'm sick of ya."

Now that I've watched it with an audience of complete strangers, that was our first test screening if you will, I said, "I'm comfortable."

Back in the day. I'd be like, "If we take out time, it's admitting failure in some stupid fuckin' way." But Quentin took *Inglourious Basterds* to Cannes and it got savaged in a bunch of places. There were people who were like, "It's not very good." Quentin went back with Sally Menke. He recut his fuckin' movie, and *Inglourious Basterds* is what it is today as we all know it. So if fuckin' Quentin Tarantino, the greatest living filmmaker in my generation, can feel that, I guess it kind of validated it for me.

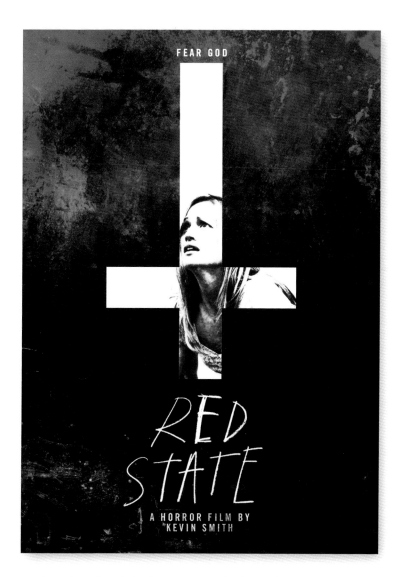

Heath Killen | Sydney, Australia | *"Red State,"* 2011

# BEN'S QUOTE

**Kevin Smith:** Two weeks ago, I reached out to [Ben] Affleck. He's a very famous filmmaker now in his own right, and he's making this movie called *Argo* back out west. It's a movie that's set in the '70s in the Iran hostage crisis. He's got a killer fuckin' cast. A lot of them came from our cast, 'cause he goes, "Hey, man, I heard a lot about *Red State*. Can you send me a DVD?"

I said, "We didn't do that. We have prints. I have two prints of the movie. You wanna borrow a print?"

"Yeah, man, we'll string it up here. Send me a print."

I sent him a print. Never heard from him again. Didn't call back to be like, "Hey, I got your print and watched it." Not even like, "Hey, I got your print." Nothing. Not a fuckin' word heard back. Then I read in one of the trades, they were like, "John Goodman cast in *Argo*." And I was like, "John Goodman. He's in *Red State* and now he's in Ben's movie." I was like, "Right on. Ben's got good taste."

Then they announced Michael Parks is gonna be in *Argo*. And I'm like, "Okay, that ain't a coincidence."

And then Kerry Bishé sent me an email going, "Just wanna thank you. I just got cast in *Argo*."

And I was like, "Motherfucker, man! That's three. He took fuckin' three. He cherry-picked three and didn't say a fuckin' word, didn't give me a hide nor hair and shit." So I reach out to Shea, his producer. I was like, "Hey man, once was kind of a coincidence. Two was a little suspicious. Fuckin' three, you might wanna have him give me a shout and fuckin' say something or anything."

She goes, "He didn't talk to you after he watched the movie?"

And I was like, "No."

And she was like, "My God, you wanna talk to him."

I was like, "You damn fuckin' skippy, I wanna talk to him."

So he sends me this fuckin' email where he's like, "Player, I heard from Shea that you didn't hear my other message." He was going, "Of course I loved your fuckin' movie, but if you didn't figure it out, didn't you pick that up when I stole half the cast?"

And so I was like, "All right, fair enough."

And so he's been working on *Argo* and whatnot. We're getting ready to run Parks for an award, which is weird to say, but Parks's performance in *Red State* is awards-worthy. So we're collecting a bunch of quotes and the one we had from Quentin—"I fucking love this movie!—Quentin Tarantino"—was so effective. It was great. We put it on the poster. "Hey man, do me a favor? You cherry-picked half the cast, Ben. Why don't you just send me over a quote I can use about the cast. Doesn't have to be about me and shit. I ain't running for nothing. But send me something that's about the cast of the movie I can put onto a poster or whatever."

And he goes, "Okay." He sent me an email back, and this was his quote—Ben Affleck, mind you, who won an Academy Award for screenwriting: "This film has an excellent cast."

So I'm like, "That's a little fuckin' dry." So I write back. I'm like, "You know what, dude? Before anyone takes that Oscar back, why don't you dig a little deeper, you know? Pretend a friend made this movie. Pretend Matt Damon made this movie. Give me a fuckin' juicier quote than that."

And he wrote back, "Ha ha ha. Sorry. Here's my real quote." And the quote was, "I fucking love this movie more than Quentin!"

Ryan Nevill | Bristol, United Kingdom | "*Red State*," 2011

# TUSK

2014

# CREATIVITY

**TELLING STORIES ON FILM** was expensive and took too long. So in 2007, Kevin Smith and Scott Mosier started podcasting for an hour a week, and one of these Internet radio shows became his eleventh film. He found a concept, a twist on '60s British Hammer horror, which at times both repulsed and intrigued him. It was the podcasts that allowed Kevin the freedom to step outside his comfort zone. It's possible he never would have even thought of directing *The Human Centipede* with a walrus. Perhaps it was this place between filmmaking and storytelling where he felt the most at home.

Because Kevin had been podcasting for so long, he had an intimate relationship with his fans. He asked them to tweet him using the hashtag #walrusyes and they agreed he should make a movie about a man who becomes a walrus. As odd and far out as this film was, his fans loved it. And what a sight to see at the Midnight Madness screening when hundreds of people showed up wearing *Tusk* masks!

Justin Long as Wallace recording the *Not-See Party* podcast, 2014
*AF Archive / Demarest Films / Alamy Stock Photo*

# TUSK ORIGIN

**Kevin Smith:** This is a website called Gumtree, and I guess it's kind of like a Craigslist for apartments or homes. You can find living arrangements here. Someone seeking someone but not necessarily for sex. A place to stay.

**Scott Mosier:** Oh. [*pretending to advertise a rental*] "I have a room available."

**KS:** Okay, so you're in Brighton and you're looking for a place. You wanna get out of your flat, if you will, where you are with your mates. You got flatmates you don't necessarily care for. I tell you, where we're going, this is something out of a Hammer horror film. This is how Hammer horror films begin.

**SM** [*imitates British accent*]: "I'm living with my buds, Teddy and Nicky. My name's Wallace."

**KS** [*reading from ad*]: "Hello, I am looking for a lodger in my house. Among the many things I have done in my life is to spend three years alone on St. Lawrence Island. These were perhaps the most intense and fascinating years of my life, and I was kept in companionship with a walrus whom I named Gregory. Never have I had such a fulfilling friendship with anyone, human or otherwise, and upon leaving the island, I was heartbroken. I now find myself in a large house overlooking Queen's Park and am keen to get a lodger. This is a position I am prepared to offer for free, no rent payable, on the fulfillment of some conditions. I have, over the last few months, been constructing a realistic walrus costume, which should fit most people of average proportions and allow for full and easy movement in character. To take on the position as my lodger, you must be prepared to wear the walrus suit for approximately two hours each day. I am a considerate person to share a house with, and other than playing the accordion, my tastes are easy to accommodate." What's the worst of it? Catching fish in my mouth?

**SM:** Only for two hours a day. Maybe he's not crazy.

**KS:** No. I don't think he's crazy. But it's a situation to keep an eye on. I would like to follow up on this and be like, "Whatever happened to your walrus buddy?" [*imitates deep British accent*] "He disappeared."

Anyone listening to this, copyright Kev and Scott because this is a fuckin' horror movie. The walrus and the carpenter. And it's about a dude who his whole life he was an architect. He's made a lot of money building houses for people. His philosophy is, "I've spent a lifetime making people happy. But now it's time for me. And what I want is very simple." And what he does is create this subterranean dungeon that looks like a fuckin' walrus enclave.

**SM:** He goes down there and presses a button. And then lights come on and then you hear seagulls and stuff . . .

**KS:** You come back to man's world and you're like, "It was better when the only person I had to talk to was a walrus." He even says it, dude. Quote, "Never have I had such a fulfilling friendship with anyone, human or otherwise. And upon leaving the island, I was heartbroken for months."

Now we're not going to make a mistake like other horror movies where they fuckin', "Meanwhile outside in the world . . ." [*imitates female British accent*] "He's supposed to meet me at the chip shop and he wasn't there."

**SM** [*imitates female British accent*]: "Where's Wallace?"

**KS:** Bullshit. The whole fuckin' movie, A, to keep it low budget, and B, because nobody cares about the outside world. But the bulk of the movie . . .

**SM:** You're in the house and you don't leave.

**KS:** He's sitting there and he's talking to the dude at this place. You do the camera thing where you look woozy and shit, and he's like, "I feel faint." And the old man's like . . .

**SM:** "It'll be all right, Gregory."

**KS:** Yeah. Fuckin' nice. So this dude goes out and when he comes back in, it's still his POV, but he's like, "Uhhh," 'cause surgery hurts and shit, I've heard. So he feels the pain of something. "Where am I? Uhhh." And then he fuckin' moves his hand and all he sees is his flipper, dude. 'Cause they have flippers, right? Little front flippers.

**SM:** Yeah, yeah, yeah. Like a walrus.

**KS:** Horrified and shit. And the [carpenter]'s like, "Ah-ha-ha-ha."

And the dude comes over and fuckin' kicks him in the face so the dude goes out. Then when he comes to again, he's in the walrus enclave.

**SM:** He hears the seagulls.

**KS:** Yes! And that's when things get horrible, dude. But if I woke up sewn together . . .

**SM:** Like a walrus.

**KS:** And this dude, the whole movie is cuddling me and shit.

**SM:** Feeding you fish.

**KS:** And when I'm not doing it, he's abusive. Not just verbally, but he fuckin' slaps me. I've got these tusks on and shit. He also does that, dude. He pulls out three of my fronts up here. He's an amateur dentist.

All right. So here's the third act. He catches you trying to escape. He gives you a fuckin' beating. You've been working at this little hole in the wall, like *Shawshank* and shit. And he fuckin' sees you. In this moment, the carpenter goes and puts on his suit. Now obviously, he can't sew his fingers shut. But he puts it on. It's still fucked-up-looking and it's made of human skins. And so you realize he's done this before, like, "I'm not the first lodger. There have been many Gregorys."

**SM:** That makes me feel bad.

**KS:** So he's in it. You're in yours, and you have to have one of them walrus fights, like on the beach, where you're slamming each other.

**SM:** So I beat him?

**KS:** You do.

**SM:** But then, what has to happen at the end is that once he makes that switch, he can't go back. So even mentally, he's crossed.

**KS:** That's our last shot, dude. We fade out or dissolve to fuckin' Havencroft Clinic for the Criminally Insane, or something like that. And you see his buddy in the beginning of the movie. Nick or fuckin' Teddy, one of those cats [*imitates hooligan British accent*], "He wound up as a walrus, didn't he?"

**SM:** He's got something wrapped in a newspaper and you don't know what's going on and then he opens it . . .

**KS:** Yes. And it's a fish. Oh, this is awesome. So the dude, Teddy, looks at him fuckin' sadly, and he's just screeching down below. And then he throws him the fish. They start playing some sad piano music. Roll credits as we pull back overhead as we watch him fuckin' eating this fish off the ground. And there's a song that's just like, "Being Tender in Your Heart."

**SM:** Is that a real song?

**KS:** No. In those fuckin' horror movies, they would end with a really mellow song that was like, "What does this have to do with eating fuckin' human brains?"

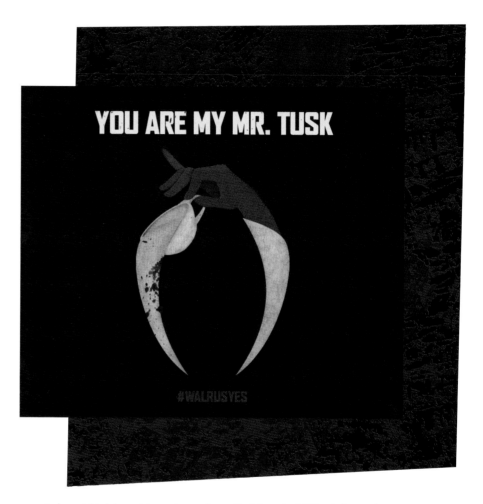

Adam Webber | Los Angeles, California | *"Tusk* Social Graphic," 2014

Top: *Tusk* at TIFF
(Toronto International
Film  Festival), 2014
*Courtesy of Nancy Taylor*

Right: Crowd of *Tusk* masks, 2014
*Courtesy of Sandy Lum*

TIFF Programmer Colin Geddes, with Kevin, Justin Long, Genesis Rodriguez,
and Haley Joel Osment at the Midnight Madness screening, 2014
*Courtesy of Ian Goring*

# Yoga Hosers

2016

# PARENTAL LOVE

**KEVIN SMITH CONTINUED HIS** True North trilogy, setting his twelfth film in Winnipeg, Canada (and ending with the yet-to-be-filmed *Moose Jaws*). Although the title was borrowed from a podcast, the horror comedy is really about girls who love yoga and must defeat a villain, the Goalie Golem, a hockey-playing monster created by a Nazi mad scientist. But it was getting to work with his daughter Harley that makes the story come full circle for Kevin. She doesn't talk about blowjobs or necrophilia, but she hates her job and wants to be dead. With her friend Lily-Rose, these clerks, like the original ones, are just trying to get to the end of the day.

Kevin has a long history with Canada, having attended film school in Vancouver, British Columbia. He loves hockey, Gretzky, and the Edmonton Oilers. So, as a true Canadaphile, even though the film was shot in Los Angeles, it's no surprise that he re-created Manitoba so faithfully. By wearing his ever-present hockey jersey, he also showed how he's a fan of Canada. Kevin's fan appeal is international, as can be seen from the many fan artists in this book. They come from all over the world, including Argentina, Australia, Chile, Denmark, Hungary, Mexico, New Zealand, Portugal, Russia, Spain, the United Kingdom, and Canada, of course.

Kevin on set, with Lily-Rose Depp as Colleen Collette and Harley Quinn Smith as Colleen McKenzie, 2015
*Pictorial Press Ltd / Alamy Stock Photo*

# WORKING WITH HARLEY

**Kevin Smith:** I had this very weird snap-to-reality moment where I was like, "Okay. All this time, twenty years in, you're convinced it was your epic journey. You're doing all this, and you're the hero of your own story in the epic novel of your life." And in that moment, as I was watching the take, I was like, "Holy shit! All of this, twenty years, has not been about me. It's been in preparation for the moment when I could be on a set with my fifteen-year-old daughter and talk to her professionally and communicate exactly what I need to after twenty years of learning how to be a director."

# ROGUE COP

**Kevin Smith:** I can tell you a story. Last time we were here at FandomFest, it was 2013. I believe we had *Super Groovy Cartoon Movie* with us. So after we screened the movie that Jason wrote and produced and starred in, we did a Q&A. Somebody asked a question that I saw a reaction come out of him—never saw fuckin' happen before in my life. He was so serious, it was crazy. Somebody in the audience goes, "Hey man, if you weren't doing what you do, like if you weren't Jay for a living, if you'd never played Jay and shit, what would you like to have done with your life?"

And without missing a beat, as if he'd been waiting his whole life to answer the question, Jason spit this response out: "Rogue cop." So I was like, "Really?" I said, "Why a rogue cop?" And he goes, "I can't play by their rules."

So we were going to make this movie called *Yoga Hosers*, which spins off of *Tusk*. There was a part for Detective Garman—Ralph Garman, friend of mine, does *Hollywood Babble-On* with me. He was in *Tusk*, very minor part, Detective Garman. In *Yoga Hosers*, he was going to get an upgrade to Commissioner Garman, and so he was going to come back; and at one point, he shows the Johnny Depp character, Guy Lapointe, to an interrogation room. But Michael Parks, who was supposed to play the villain in the third act, was sick while we were making the movie. So I had to swap him out with somebody else; and I moved Ralph Garman up, so Ralph Garman plays the villain in the third act of the movie. I'm losing the scene with Ralph altogether. And I was going to just start with Guy Lapointe in the interrogation room. I remember this sad sack and he was like, "I just want to act with Johnny Depp." Little fuckin' match girl. And so, not wanting to break his heart, I was like, "Let me see if I can fuckin' jam him in here." You can't be Commissioner Garman, but maybe I can just fuckin' make him a cop. And I was like, "Wait a second, man." I remembered fuckin' Louisville, Kentucky, two years ago when a little boy stood on stage and said these two words, "Rogue cop." So I changed it with one word.

You will see a scene where one of the world's greatest actors, Johnny Depp, interacts with one of the world's actors, Mr. Jason Mewes. And I'll be honest with you, it has one of my favorite Mewes moments in cinema history. It's very simple.

Guy Lapointe has written a book referencing the events in *Tusk*, so there's a running joke in the movie that it was a complete failure and all the critics hated it. So this guy, his character, the rogue cop, he's holding the book. We're in the interrogation room with the two girls. All of a sudden, the door opens and you see this guy, and he's looking around and he waves in Guy Lapointe. Guy Lapointe comes in and he says, "I can't thank you enough for doing this," to Jay.

And Jay's just like, "No, no, no. You got a few minutes, man. Don't worry about it." And he goes, "This," he holds up Guy Lapointe's book, "this is my Bible," and that was all he was supposed to say and then leave the room, presumably to go stall other police and shit.

So we do the takes and I get what I need. And I'm like, "Dude, I'm happy. I got what I need. I'm moving on."

And he goes, "Whoa, whoa, whoa. Can we do one more?" And I go, "Why?" And he goes, "I want to try doing it as a Canadian."

So we do the take. And it plays exactly as we did [before]. He comes in the room, looks around, waves in Guy Lapointe. Guy Lapointe comes into the room. And he goes, "I'll give you a few minutes. I'll stall them."

And Guy Lapointe goes, "I don't know how to thank you for doing this."

And Jay goes, "No, no. Don't worry about it, man. This book is my Bible." Then he steps back and he goes, "And you're like a Goddamn Canadian Batman, eh?"

Marina Cardoso Fernandes | Ryazan, Russia | "Guy Lapointe *Yoga Hosers*," 2016

**KEVIN SMITH**

*Yoga Hosers*, featuring songbirdcosplay, 2017
*Courtesy of Tascha Dearing*

Pernille Ørum | Copenhagen, Denmark | "Yoga Hosers," 2016

Will Perkins | Rochester, New York | *Yoga Hosers* VHS," 2019 Courtesy of Alex DiVincenzo

# REFERENCES TO CLERKS

**Kevin Smith:** Most of the time, it's in a convenience store in Canada, Eh-2-Zed, the one that was in *Tusk*. Once we were back in convenience-store world, I couldn't not make a few *Clerks* references and stuff like that. And my favorite is when my kid screams, "I'm not even supposed to be here today!" That, to me, was a really sweet moment on set 'cause, number 1, I was happy she nailed the line and I could put it into the movie and it works in the scene and stuff. So even if you don't know *Clerks*, it still kind of works in the movie.

But as the guy that did *Clerks* twenty-one years later, to be standing in a different convenience store in a different part of the world and my kid was saying the line, I couldn't have predicted that shit. I couldn't have predicted any of this, where it all went. I just wanted to see *Clerks*, that was it. And because I made that movie, it kind of took me on this weird journey, and the journey gets weirder the older I get 'cause now I'm at a place where I do shit just to watch people's expressions change. I don't sit there and go, "What's good for my career?" Clearly not. Now I sit there and go, "What would I like to do? What's fucked up that I would like to see? What doesn't exist?" and stuff like that.

So, for me to be in the convenience store, I had to throw in references, as many as I could. And there's hidden ones in there as well. There's a Chewlies gum ad I guess is pretty out in front of everybody. Yeah, I guess I'll never escape convenience-store movies. If I live to be eighty-two, I will die in a convenience store, shooting some movie about a convenience store. And that'd be okay, man. I'd be all right with that.

mischakiddo | Austin, Texas | "Sorry Aboot That," 2017

# HARLEY

# NOSTALGIA

**FOR HIS THIRTEENTH FILM,** Kevin Smith decided to revisit his most iconic characters. And he cherry-picked cast members from all of his previous films and fucked with his mythology, even giving Jay a daughter. It had been more than twenty-five years since *Clerks*, and he was still making films about ordinary people in his extraordinary world.

Kevin re-embraced the interconnected universe that he had created so long ago. And after he survived his heart attack, his fans were there to support him and show their love. He got to do his own View Askew scrapbook. After all those years of filmmaking, it was like going to his twenty-fifth reunion, where they could relive memories and share all that goodwill that had sustained him over his entire career.

# THE RETURN OF JAY AND SILENT BOB

KEVIN POSTED THIS ON INSTAGRAM, FEBRUARY 9, 2017, ANNOUNCING THAT HE HAD FINISHED A SCRIPT FOR A SEQUEL TO *JAY AND SILENT BOB STRIKE BACK*.

@jayandsilentbob are coming back! Here's the story: Sadly, Clerks III can't happen (one of our four leads opted out of the flick). So I worked on a #Mallrats movie instead... which also didn't happen because it turned into a #Mallrats series. I've pitched said sequel series to 6 different networks only to find no takers thus far. Mind you, I'm not complaining: nobody gets to make EVERYTHING they wanna make in this business (do they?). And I've been lucky to make anything at all, there's so much competition out there, so many much cooler ideas from fresh folks. And besides: I had #comicbookmen and then @tuskthemovie and @yogahosers (which all came together so crazy quickly), and the podcasts and #fatmanonbatman. With all of that, how could I bitch about no Clerks III or Mallrats 2? Then when I started directing @thecw shows, it was such a slice of Heaven on Earth, I happily put my Askewniverse sequels to the side. Since I sold #Clerks and #Mallrats years ago, they're owned by others, which limits my moves with my own material. I don't mind: back in the day, all I

ever wanted to do was sell my stuff so I could be in the movie biz in the first place. So I don't own Clerks, Mallrats, Chasing Amy or #Dogma... But I DO own #jayandsilentbob. So while I love playing with someone else's new toys on @cwtheflash and @Supergirl, I'm getting eager to play with my old toys again in the inter-connected View Askewniverse I spent the first half of my career creating. And so all last month, I had the time of my life laughing while writing "Jay and Silent Bob Reboot" - a fun flick in which the Jersey boys have to go back to Hollywood to stop a brand new reboot of the old "Bluntman & Chronic Movie" they hated so much. It's a tongue-in-cheek, silly-ass satire that pokes fun at the movie business's recent re-do obsession, featuring an all-star cast of cameos and familiar faces! And I already met with the good folks at Miramax and they're into it, so I'm hoping we'll be shooting in the summer! Never give up, kids. You CAN do anything you want in life, so long as you're patient and malleable. #KevinSmith

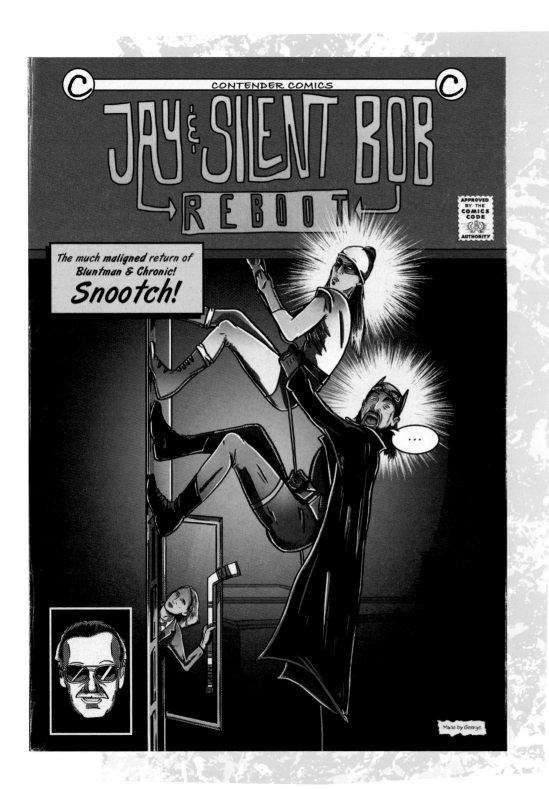

"One of my all time favourite directors, writers, story tellers and humans is Kevin Smith. I watched his films as a teen and still to this day. Taking inspiration from Smith's love of comics and Batman, this is a homage to the 1960s Adam West, Burt Ward Batman and Robin with a little Stan Lee 'non-refundable barcode' cameo in there for good measure."

–George Katralis

George Katralis l London, United Kingdom l "Jay and Silent Bob Reboot," 2019

Phaserunner | United Kingdom |
"Jay and Silent Bob: Reboot – VHS,"
2019

**KEVIN SMITH**

Justin Morales | Tennessee | "Jay and Silent Bob Reboot," 2019

# STRIP-MINING THE SEQUELS

**David Gati:** Can you talk about deciding to write *Jay and Silent Bob Reboot*? Basically, tell the story from the beginning.

**Kevin Smith:** *Reboot* had a fraught road to realization. It started as *Clerks III*, and we got real close to *Clerks III*, so much so that we started crewing up and we were going to be shooting in Philly, or outside of Philadelphia. But we were using *Creed*'s crew. *Creed* had just got done shooting, and a lot of our crew was coming from that movie. So we were a month out from leaving, and then the whole thing fell apart 'cause one of the cast members didn't want to do it. That was very frustrating, to be so close and then suddenly have it stop. So then I was like, "Well you know what, man, *Clerks III* was largely set outside of a mall." So I was like, "We had scouted malls; we found a mall. And so why don't I just do *Mallrats* instead?" And I asked my agent, "Could I do a *Mallrats* sequel? Universal has it. Do I need them to do it? Can I get the rights back?" And he told me there were three ways in which *Mallrats 2* would get made.

He said, "One, Universal just wants to pay for it themselves. That's the best possible way. Two, Universal wants to co-finance it, so we'd go out and find indie money, and they'd put in some money. Or three, they don't want to finance it at all, but they let you take the title and you go make your sequel."

"Anyway, I'm making that movie."

He said, "Yes."

And so I started writing *Mallrats 2*. I started collecting everybody in the cast, and up on Instagram I was throwing up pictures of everyone holding up two fingers, steamrolling toward what I felt would be, "We could start in March." I already had a mall scoped out, and we were probably going to just stay in Pennsylvania, which is where *Clerks III* was going to be 'cause we'd already set up everything.

And then my agent said, "Uh, Universal has to see the script." I said, "Why?" He said, "They have to make sure that you don't, you know, make fun of them or degrade their company in any sort of way."

So I was like, "Oh, all right." 'Cause it's not like we made any jokes like, "Remember the Holocaust? Universal Pictures was responsible for that."

So then it was three or four days later, my agent goes, " Um . . . we got a thing."

I said, "What's the thing? He's like, "Universal doesn't want to make the movie." I'm like, "Great. And they probably don't want to co-finance it, so we get to go make it ourselves. I'd rather do it that way. I get it. They don't give a shit. They're *Fast & Furious*. We're old and wrinkled."

And he goes, "No, Universal considers themselves a catalogue company, like a company that has old movies. Yes, they make new movies, but they're more of a catalogue company. All their IP, their library, is what they're based on; their worth is based on that." So he said, "In

Kevin and David pose together after the interview at Kevin's house, 2019. *Courtesy of Sally Gati*

the history of Universal films, they've never released a title, ever. They've never given somebody back a movie."

So I was like, "So what are you saying, man? You said, 'There are three ways in which this happens.' And now there's only two, and right now they don't want to do it." So I'm like, "I just spent all this time writing a script and collecting the cast and all that stuff." So at that point, double frustration, 'cause I couldn't make *Clerks III* and I couldn't make *Mallrats 2*. Problem is, they were both owned by different entities. I created the originals, but somebody else owned them. So I did own and still own Jay and Silent Bob. Me and Jay together own those characters. We were able to secure those characters when we made our *Clerks* deal. It was after our *Clerks* deal, actually papering it, [which] was written on yellow legal pad up at Sundance in January of '94.

But then, when we got down from the mountain, they actually put together a legit contract, with ink and stuff like that. So when they did that, I'd said to my lawyer, "I know I want to use Jay and Silent Bob in *Mallrats*. I'm going to write them in, and I know I had them in the script for *Dogma*, so is there any way to keep them out of the contract or something like that?"

He goes, "I'll just ask for the rights to those characters, see what happens." So he went to Miramax and was like, "Kevin Smith wants to retain the rights to the Jay and Silent Bob characters in the movie *Clerks*."

And Miramax was like, "Well, the movie's called *Clerks*, about the guys who were clerks, not the dudes outside the store. Go ahead."

So I got to keep those characters, which is insanely rare, and those characters did become kind of popular. And every time I put them in a movie, they became more popular; and eventually we made *Jay and Silent Bob Strike Back*. They had their own movie. They were even in *Clerks II*. They were in other people's movies. Popped up in *Scream 3* and stuff. And honestly I live in this house probably largely because of Jay and Silent Bob. So they wound up to be very valuable, and I own them, along with Jason. I owned them for a long time myself; and then when Jason got clean, I was like, "Now you can own yourself again." 'Cause back when he was doing drugs, he'd have given himself away for a needle and stuff. So that's where Jordan comes in. Jordan, Jason's wife, runs our company. You know, she helped him become super-responsible, and she's the one that knows that like, "Oh, this is a business that he's just neglected his whole life, 'cause he didn't understand that he is himself for a living."

So after those two movies didn't happen and me sitting around going, "Well, we own Jay and Silent Bob. That means we can make a Jay and Silent Bob movie and nobody can stop us. So, fuck it. I'm gonna make a Jay and Silent Bob movie." So I started to write *Jay and Silent Bob Reboot*. And it was made up of pieces of *Clerks III* and *Mallrats 2*. So the opening scene of *Clerks III* is the opening scene of *Jay and Silent Bob Reboot* minus Randal and Elias, [who] was also in the opening scene in *Clerks III*. The ending sequence, the third act of *Jay and Silent Bob Reboot*, is largely lifted in parts from the third act of *Mallrats 2*, including Iron Bob. And mind you, I also tried to turn *Mallrats* into a TV series. Like, we pitched it to Netflix, Hulu, Showtime . . .

And I got so frustrated, 'cause each time you'd walk into the room, I'd get, "Oh my God, I love *Mallrats*. It's my religion." And you'd pitch them *Mallrats 2* as a series, and they'd be like, "All right, we'll let you know." And then you'd get a phone call in an hour from your agent going like, "They're not into it."

I'm like, "I thought they loved this shit."

So after trying to push it forward, finally I was like, "You know what . . . Jay and Silent Bob." So I'd strip-mined my favorite parts of *Mallrats* that made sense for *Jay and Silent Bob Reboot* and kind of repurposed them and put 'em in there.

So I had a script. You'd have to go on Instagram to see. I put it up one day, the front page of the script. I think that was two and a half years ago at this point, and announced, "We're doing this." And you know, we weren't anywhere close to doing it. Because I'd written a script, yes, that was the first big step, but we didn't have any money. We had no leads. We were just willing it out there.

A big part of my career was, sometimes you just got to say it, and that forces you to do it. You throw your hat over the wall. You just kind of do the Babe Ruth, where you point to the far left field or right field or whatever.

You just gotta follow fucking through, because then if you don't, you look like an asshole. All you're risking is reputation and shit; but if your reputation matters to you, then you tend to have to follow through. It forces you to do what you have to do, to do the thing that you want to do. So I was like, "This is what we're doing next. *Jay and Silent Bob Reboot*."

And it took two years to get to [the point] when we actually shot the movie. Including, you know, some of that time I'd been felled by a heart attack, so I was out of the picture for a few months because of that. But that didn't make raising money for the movie any easier. Suddenly, you're a health risk as well.

We had a financier drop out. That's a problem when you're piece-mealing a budget together. If you don't have the money yourself and you're turning to others, you're at the mercy of others. So we had a deal going, and all of a sudden it fell through at the last minute—which, honestly, afforded me an opportunity to kind of step in and invest in my own art, which, you know, that's how I got started in the first place. So rather than let that be a problem, like, "You know what, 'I'll gamble my house on this,'" 'cause I knew it would work. I knew we'd get our money back at the very least, so I thought we'd do some business.

So once we had that, Universal signed on for international rights, Saban Films signed on for domestic rights. That's the majority of our budget there. Then we have some outside financing, equity financing as they call it. It came from Hideout Pictures, from Skitbags. Yeah, and those are the outside investors.

**DG:** Cool.

**KS:** So we had loot and we were kinda ready to go at that point.

# NEW ORLEANS: RE-CREATING QUICK STOP

**Kevin Smith:** And then the big discussion was, "Where do we shoot?" Louisiana was cheap. They got a rebate program there. So it was Louisiana, Atlanta, somewhere in a state that gives a 25–30 percent tax rebate. That was where we were going to be going; but in my head and heart, I was going, "Yeah, but we begin and end the movie at the Quick Stop, so we will definitely be going to New Jersey, 'cause that's what we did on *Jay and Silent Bob Strike Back*. We shot the whole thing out in Los Angeles, California, but then went home to shoot the Quick Stop stuff in New Jersey. So we wrapped the movie back in New Jersey. So I expected, "Oh, we'll do the same thing here."

The big difference was, on *Jay and Silent Bob Strike Back* in the year 2001, we made that movie for $20 million, and *Jay and Silent Bob Reboot*, $10 million. So you don't get to do the exact same thing. I'm not saying that's why there's no orangutan in the movie. Really, you don't put an orangutan in the movie, because now if you use a real orangutan, you'd be skinned by people that are animal-rights activists. You'd have to do a CG orangutan, and that would be cost prohibitive for a dopey movie like ours. So, some things fall away from the story, and allow for you to do it less expensive. Going to New Jersey was a $500,000 expense, which is 5 percent of your budget. And then you have to decide, how important is it?

A fan artist's re-creation of Quick Stop (scratch-built 1:25 scale miniature created from MDF, wood, cardboard, plastic card, chalk pastels, acrylic paint, wire, plastruct) Joshua Smith | Norwood, Australia | "Quickstop Groceries," 2018

Now, at the beginning of the process, I was like, "It's everything, and I'll quit this movie if we don't go back to New Jersey to shoot because you can't duplicate the Quick Stop. It's a well-known cinematic fuckin' landmark."

And then when push came to shove and we got down to Louisiana, they said, "Nate [Jones]," who was the production designer, "he's real good, man. He thinks he can duplicate the Quick Stop."

And I was like, "You can't duplicate the Quick Stop. It's a one-of-a-kind building. It's impossible. You can't do that." I forgot that I had worked in the movie business where they made the *Titanic* and then sank it again. I mean, you can do any fuckin' thing. But I was just like, "What? Replicate a concrete block from New Jersey, one of the ugliest buildings, with no architectural fuckin' design or flair whatsoever? Impossible!"

So they took me to a building in Louisiana, outside New Orleans. And they'd shown me a mock-up. They took a picture of this building and then put up a Quick Stop sign on it and fake doors. And you know, I'm like, "Oh . . . well, yeah! It looks like it in a fuckin' picture that's doctored, but what about real life?" So they took me out to the location. And the location of the building itself, the architecture . . . it was almost as if the same people had designed the same two buildings. Like, squat, square, ugly, functional at best—the only way to describe it, man. Nobody's sitting here going, like, "Let's give 'em something to look at." Just fuckin' functional as fuck. That's all it was. This place has a dry cleaners in it. The door placement is completely different, so you have to kind of pull that idea out of your brain and just stand back and look at the building itself.

So I'm lookin' at the building and I'm like, "Wow! It's kinda the same shape. And yeah, I guess if you hung some doors here. The steel shutters are closed, and we don't have to put up no windows anyway." And only the texture of the building was different. You'd have to get real fuckin' close, and you'd have to know those movies like I know those movies. But while the structure was the same, the texture of the building was brick. It was painted, but it was brick; whereas Quick Stop is one giant wall of stucco hell. So, you know, I was like, "Well, yeah, man. Like, honestly, you might be able to make this work." I was like,

"But the brick—that's just not what the Quick Stop's made of. But we'll paint it, so it don't matter."

And Nate was like, "I'll put a skin on it." I was like, "What's that?" And he was like, "Just a fake front. We're in the movie business." And I was like, "All right."

So I went the day we went to shoot the movie. I saw the thing, and we put a video up of it, like a behind-the-scenes video that we shot, and I was just dumbfounded. They were somehow able to replicate that building, like it looked exactly like the Quick Stop in my memory, not the Quick Stop of real life. They've got these weird pylons to stop you from driving through the store. I guess somebody went through the window. It's a park-and-blockade thing. And the color's different now. But the one that I saw looked exactly like the one I remembered. So I started crying. "Oh my God, I can't believe you did it." So that allowed us to stay in Louisiana and not spend half a million for one day to go to New Jersey and shoot the Quick Stop.

## FINDING THE CAST

**Kevin Smith:** We started production one year to the date of my heart attack. So if I had a heart attack on February 26, 2018, we started shooting February 26, 2019. Me and Jay were the only two hundred-percent-confirmed cast members when we went down to New Orleans. We had yeses from Melissa Benoist. She told me yes, like years prior, always in the same role. She was always meant to play Chronic. Diedrich Bader, who played the security guard that runs around the lot in *Jay and Silent Bob Strike Back*, he said yes. And Jason Biggs, who was returning to play Jason Biggs. So those were the only three that were locked and confirmed, along with me, Jason, and Harley, my daughter, 'cause she plays Jason's daughter in the movie. And that was it. Everyone else we had to cast.

Now I knew I wanted Aparna [Brielle], who plays Jihad, to join us. She's friends with Harley. So I'd met her. "Oh, she'd be great in the flick."

**KEVIN SMITH**

Treshelle [Edmond] plays Sopapilla. Alice [Wen] plays Shan Yu. They're part of Millie's girl gang. And Jennifer was pretty locked too; my wife Jennifer's in the movie. I knew I could count on her to be in the movie as well 'cause she was going to be down there anyway. Everyone else we didn't have locked.

And the scary thing was [that] we told Universal and Saban Films, "We're going to get all the cameos." 'Cause that's what people remember about *Jay and Silent Bob Strike Back*; it's full of cameos. And it's easy to get cameos when you shoot here in Los Angeles 'cause it's where everybody fuckin' lives. But we had moved down to shoot our picture in Louisiana. And, yeah, they shoot movies and TV there, but here, we could call up [Ben] Affleck and Mattie [Damon] and just be like, "Hey, man, can you come down to Sweetzer? We're shooting this scene. It's like four minutes from your place. We'll get you out of here in an hour." You can't do that in Louisiana. It's much further away.

So we thought we were fucked. And then what happened was we shot the movie during Mardi Gras. And when you'd call cast members to be like, "Hey, man, do you want to come down to New Orleans for a day to shoot one scene? It's gonna take like two hours."

They're like, "You want to fly me down to New Orleans during Mardi Gras? Oh, fuck yeah. I'll take a free trip to Mardi Gras." And they all came down.

And the ones that weren't convinced by Mardi Gras, I guilted them into it. So you know, you call 'em up and be like, "Hey, man, you want to be in the movie?" And they're like, "Nah, I don't know, man. New Orleans is kinda far and shit." And I'd be like, "You do remember I almost died, right?" And they'd be like, "All right, man. I'm coming, I'm coming."

So I had a very guilty cast. I used the heart attack. That was my casting agent. So we got a bunch of people to show up. And the credits for *Jay and Silent Bob Strike Back*, it's like twenty-two or twenty-five end cards of faces. We were worried we wouldn't even be near that for *Reboot*. When *Reboot* was done, we had double that: we had forty-four different cards at the end of the movie for the cast.

*On July 20, 2019, Kevin went to San Diego Comic-Con Hall H and told this story about Ben Affleck returning to the View Askewniverse.*

**Kevin Smith:** Ben, I never reached out to and didn't even write him into the movie originally, 'cause I hadn't spoken to him in, like, eight years at that point. You know, *Jay and Silent Bob Strike Back*, Ben played Ben Affleck and he also played Holden McNeil. In this, there was going to be no Ben Affleck and no Ben Affleck jokes, and there was going to be no Holden McNeil or anything like that. As you see, Brodie in this movie takes the job that Holden kind of had in the last movie, where he sets the boys on their mission. That's how resolute I felt. He's not coming back, and so I didn't even build him into it.

But [entertainment journalist] Kevin McCarthy was sitting down with Ben to do an interview for a junket for Netflix, this movie called *Triple Frontier* that Ben was in. So Kevin McCarthy, his first thing off the bat, he just says to Ben as a warmup, "Hey, have they called you for *Reboot* yet?"

And Ben goes, "No, they haven't, and I'm available."

And our world stopped! Everyone in production, because it was on Twitter, [was] like, "Did you fucking see this?"

And I was like, "Oh, oh, that's nice. That's some nice shit you say at a junket." People say shit to me all the time, and I'm like, "Yeah, of course," but inside I'm like, "I hate that prick." That's not worth following up on.

And they were like, "You should. You should really poke around. Why don't you reach out to him, call him?"

I was like, "I haven't worked with him since *Clerks II*." He hadn't been in one of our flicks. I thought our friendship was dead. And I never wanted to reach out and find out I was right. You know, it's one thing to think this motherfucker just don't like me anymore 'cause I never hear from this person. It's another thing to have that confirmed. If you're like, "Hey, motherfucker, do you like me anymore?" And they're like, "Fuck no." And suddenly you're carrying that like a cross for the rest of your life. So it's better to live in ignorance. Ignorance was bliss.

And so my people were pushing me to pop that balloon of ignorance and potentially open myself up to harm, to heartbreak and shit. And I've had enough fuckin' heartbreak, so I'm like, "I don't want to fuckin' do that. I ain't gonna bother the guy. We got our plans. We got a movie to make, and everything's going fine. We got the money for this movie without him. We don't need Holden to tell this story. We're doing just fine. I'm not reaching out."

And we made the movie for another week. And then they kept poking me and I kept ignoring it. And then it just started to sit on my chest. It wasn't about the movie. I was just scared. I just didn't want to be rejected. I didn't want to reach out and find out for sure that he was like, "Fuck you." Because I'd always wondered, "All those years we made those movies, didn't they mean anything? They meant something to me. Didn't they mean anything to him? We never hear from him anymore." So I never wanted to reach out.

Finally, I write this tweet that I'm going to send. And thankfully Jordan, Jay's wife, producer on the movie, right before I sent it, she read it. And she said, "Don't tweet that. Just text it to him." And I was like, "I've got a bunch of old numbers. They probably don't work. That'd be weird and invasive to send him a text." She's going, "It'd be a weird attack to send him a tweet in public and shit."

I was like, "Good point. Good point." And so I texted him, and this is what I texted. I texted a bunch of shit, and I won't read you that. But I closed up—and it's relevant to this room 'cause it's from fuckin' *Conan the Barbarian*—I said, "But to paraphrase the sad old King Osric in *Conan the Barbarian*, 'There comes a time when the jewels cease to sparkle, when the gold loses its luster, when the throne room becomes a prison, and all that's left is the director's love for the people he used to make pretend with.'" And I sent him that text, and I fuckin' waited with a clenched asshole. Last time I spoke to my friend, I was a different person altogether. You know, I was "that Kevin Smith." Now I'm "'that'

Kevin Smith." And I've mellowed out incredibly. I've always been fairly mellow, but fuckin' once I'd become a stoner ten years ago, Jesus Christ, I have no pulse whatsoever, man. You know, very little gets me upset or excited. So I run deep and hard, and I was afraid that the thing I'd said to him, like quoting Conan, "What the fuck is wrong with you? It's no wonder I haven't reached out to this fool."

But my old friend, who I came up with, who I'd shared creative DNA with, who I'd dreamt with, who slept on my fuckin' couch while we made *Chasing Amy*, who I first saw in *Mallrats* and was just like, "Why aren't you a fuckin' leading man, man? You're charming and funny and shit, funniest fuckin' dude I know. You should be the lead in movies. I'm gonna write you a fuckin' lead in a movie." The guy that I met the first day in an audition for *Mallrats*, I'd just read about him and his buddy selling a script to Castle Rock in the Hollywood Reporter. "Hey, man. Congratulations. I read you guys sold a spec script."

And he looked at me shocked, like, "How do you fuckin' know that?" I was like, "Oh," I said, "I read the trades."

He goes, "You care about that shit?" I was like, "Yeah, I like the entertainment business. Entertainment journalism fascinates me. Congratulations."

And he goes, "You're a fuckin' fan, aren't you?"

I just met the fuckin' guy, man, and right away I knew that I liked him. That guy, who I hadn't reached out to for all that time 'cause I was terrified of what he'd say, he wrote back this, and it was so perfectly Ben. Ben wrote back, "Of course you still liken yourself to a king."

And right then and there, I felt safe. I felt so safe. I was like, "Oh my God. I don't care what he says next. I don't care if he says he's busy for the next ten years. The guy I used to joke around with just texted me the way we used to talk to each other. You got to understand, the ending of our relationship predated SMS. I don't think I ever shared a text with Ben Affleck. I framed that shit, like it meant the world to me. So I said, "Do you want to come out and play? We're all having a blast in the past, man." And he said, "I would love to."

And he came out. Not only did he come out to do the flick—I didn't know what to cast him in 'cause we'd cast everything. There was nothing really left, but I was like, "Maybe I can make up a part. Maybe I could stick him in this scene or something like that." All of it seemed like a waste because he was coming. He didn't even make us do it in L.A.

He's like, "Oh, I'll come to New Orleans."

And so he was making the trip. So I was like, "Fuck it." I fell asleep one night, thinking about it. I was like, "Jesus, man, I hadn't seen him in eight years and he's willing to get on a plane and come down here and shoot the scene. We don't even know what it is." I said, "I should do something special. Fuck." So next morning, I texted him. I was like, "Would you mind playing Holden again?"

And he was like, "I was hoping you would say that."

And so I said, "All right, give me a minute. I think I can come up with something." And I wrote an eight-page sequel to *Chasing Amy* that just follows up twenty years later and functions perfectly within the movie. If you see the movie, you'll be like, "Wait, that scene didn't exist when you started the fuckin' movie? Why would you have bothered?" It is the emotional culmination of the movie and sends us into a really great place.

So he came and did the scene. It's, like, eight pages. And when I sent him the scene, first thing he texted back was like, "Bro, I have not done this much dialogue in the last three movies I was in."

And I was like, "Too much?"

He goes, "No. I think I can handle it." But my favorite thing that he wrote was, "You've changed. There's an awful lot of italics in my shit now." And I had to explain. I was like, "Because now I write in a computer program, not a typewriter, and I can italicize shit."

So Affleck says he's coming and I didn't know who I was getting, right? I assumed I'd get the Ben Affleck that made *Argo*, for Christ

sakes. I didn't know if I'd get Batman, but I knew I'd at least get the director, the fucking guy who knows how to make a film. Last time we'd worked together, he hadn't even made *Gone Baby Gone*. He'd directed some shorts, but he hadn't directed a feature, so I didn't know who was going to get off the plane, join us on set. I was like, "Man, if Holden shows up at all, this is a win."

So he comes. I see him for the first time in years. I fuckin' hug him and melt in his arms and cry.

He goes, "You smoke too much weed now, man."

I said, "Am I overly emotional?"

He goes, "You were always a crier."

So we chitchatted. We got to know each other again. Then we went to set 'cause we were on a schedule. It was the last day of the movie. All of this happened on the last day of production. We had to shoot eight pages, and we had five other scenes to do. We go for blocking. Joey [Lauren Adams] is there as well. So they're working together for the first time since fuckin' *Chasing Amy*. Jason's there and I'm there. So the four of us were there in 1996, when we made that fuckin' movie. We all hugged and bonded.

And then I sent everyone else on the crew away so we could have a blocking rehearsal just by ourselves, which was the way we used to do in the old days. It's just the actors and the director. So we go for the blocking, very simple blocking. We walk into a room and fuckin' stand there. Joey has her sides, which is a small version of the script in her hands. Jason has his sides 'cause he's got a lot of dialogue. I had my sides and I'm Silent Bob and I have no lines, but I still had a set of sides in my hand. Ben didn't have his sides. So it was like, "Do you want a set of sides?" And he goes, "I think I got it."

And then I was like, "All right." We were just blocking, so it didn't matter. I was like, "So let's run the scene, top to bottom." And he fuckin' knew every line of every one of those eight pages, including a two-page fucking monologue, like verbatim and shit. He could've done the monologue backwards, completely. If I was like, "Go to the end and say it backwards," he knew every fuckin' line. I almost cried. I did cry because he was working the way we worked together back in 1996.

He got on a plane and was like, "Oh, in order to do Kevin's movie, I have to know every single word of dialogue, because that one time he yelled at us because we didn't know every word in the script," which is true. On *Chasing Amy*, we went in to rehearse one day, and Joey, Ben, and Jason were fuckin' around.

They didn't know all the words and I was like, "You know what, everyone go home. We're about to start shooting this movie, and nobody's being serious about it. Just everyone go home and read your lines. Learn your lines."

And Ben was like, "I've never seen you mad in my life."

And I was like, "That was as mad as I ever got?"

And he was like, "Yeah. You just seemed fuckin' disappointed, like a dad." So he went off and read the entire script. Learned the entire script.

So the dude who came to join us in New Orleans memorized the entire scene and had it down absolutely cold, which was insanely touching. Like I told him, "If you had given me half that shit, I would have been a happy camper."

He's like, "The words were important, bro. They were always important."

# SHOOTING IN DIGITAL TIME

**Kevin Smith:** It was a tougher shoot than I imagined it would ever be [by] virtue of the fact that I'd been directing for twenty-five years at that point. But the directing that I've been doing in the last decade since *Clerks II* hasn't really involved me on camera, with the exception of [the web series] *Hollyweed*. I'm not really the guy that ever is acting in his own stuff. And lately, I'm doing the CW shows, which I'm really not in, so I'm not used to directing the movie and directing me and being in the movie. And that slowed us down a little bit. And not because I was slower or anything. . . .

Technology, oddly enough, slowed us down. Back in the day—like, say, when we were making *Jay and Silent Bob Strike Back*—I'm in the shot, we shoot it. Then after the scene is done, I say, "Cut," and it's usually no more than a three-minute take. Then you go back to the monitor and you watch the scene and make sure that you're getting what you want and what I need for every edit. And if I don't have it, I self-correct, "All right. Hold on, one more. I just want to do one more take." You go out. You do that. Come back and watch it. "All right. That's great. Let's move on." It's three minutes and maybe the second one's a pick-up, so it's not even three minutes. It's like half of that, so it's a minute and a half. And then you're moving on.

We live in the digital age now. So, that was all about film, and you'd always cut because film is expensive as shit. You gotta process all that shit. Digital is cheap as fuck. Digital just takes time, not dime; so all it takes is the time to take it off the camera and stick it into your laptop, download the footage, then clear that card, put it back in the camera, and you're back to shooting and shit. That's camera reloading these days. So people don't cut nearly as much as they used to. Even when you're the director and you're like, "Cut!" They're like, "Still rolling. We're good." Then you'd be like, "All right."

You just keep going with it, reset to the top, 'cause they're like, "It's digital. Go. Don't worry."

Problem is, when you finally get to the end of your take, you're like, "So now I have to watch it—all fuckin' twenty minutes." 'Cause that's how I do my job. We shoot it and then I sit and watch it. So in three-minute increments, you're moving on it fast. When you gotta watch twenty fuckin' minutes, you're like, "Everybody grab a drink 'cause we're just gonna sit here and fuckin' watch. Go to the bathroom. Smoke 'em if you got 'em." And that's the process.

Film moves a lot faster than I did when we made *Jay and Silent Bob Strike Back*, and [my DP, Yaron Levy] is very nimble on his feet. So he was like, "When they brought the schedule down to twenty-five days, I honestly thought that was still too much. I was like, 'My God, we're going to finish in eighteen days.'" He's going, "But what I didn't take into consideration was [that] you are in the movie and directing the movie." And he's like, "That slows the process down."

And it's not anybody's fault. It's not a bad thing. It's just a part of the process that I've never really been accustomed to working with.

Periodically the AD [Dan Katzman] would be like, "We've gotta move on. We're just sitting around and watching."

And [Yaron] would say, "Dano, do you hear a studio screaming at you to get moving? Is the director yelling at anybody because we're behind? This is just the process now, man. So enjoy it."

'Cause in film you're like, "We gotta go! We gotta go!" But we can't go until we got it. And so I don't know if we got it till I watch it. So you gotta shoot it, then watch it.

**Kevin Smith:** Unlike in *Jay and Silent Bob Strike Back*, where me and Jay were, say in 90 percent of the movie, there are scenes we're not in—scenes with the girl gang, scenes with Will Ferrell. We are in every scene, or I should say, I am in every scene in this movie. Sometimes Jay's not with me. But I am in every scene in this movie as either Silent Bob or as Kevin Smith, and sometimes as both in one scene. So this is the big "I love myself fest." I think I can get away with it once 'cause of the heart attack.

When we did *Jay and Silent Bob Strike Back*, there were some rumblings on what was then still the early Internet about, like, "This is like just a big fan film. This is a movie just for his fans. It's just like a big expensive YouTube fan film. Why is he fuckin' making a movie about these two guys and bringing all of his other characters in?" In my head, that all made sense. We made *Clerks* in '93. It came out in '94. *Mallrats* came out in '95; [*Chasing*] *Amy* came out in '97; *Dogma* came out in '99. And we'd had this really long, nice build, a couple years build to popularity. People knew these characters, and Jay and Silent Bob were in each one of them. So it felt like—particularly after, as hardcore as some people got about *Dogma*—I just wanted to do something fun and light. Well, people loved Jay and Silent Bob in *Dogma*. Even Mattie Damon was like, "Fuckin' Jason Mewes stole the show, and I was dressed in wings, you know."

So I was like, "Maybe we lean into that. Maybe we'll do a Jay and Silent Bob movie." And so that was only seven years after I made my first film. And I guess that was too soon for some cats to be looking back on my career, being nostalgic or doing a victory lap or something like that—which you could make the argument, fine. Now, though, twenty-five years into my career, this is the perfect time. This is a movie that's about my characters and me and my podcasting and my life and my kid who plays Jason's kid, and Jason's kid plays Ben's kid.

It's a flick that's a big scrapbook of my entire life. 'Cause when I was on the table having a heart attack . . . when the doctor was like, "You're having a widow-maker, man," he goes, "You know what that is?" I said, "No."

He said, "You're a comic-book guy. You're gonna love this. Widow-maker is the artery that goes across the front of your heart, man. That's the LAD. You've got a hundred percent blockage in the LAD, so nothing is getting through. That's why you're suffering this heart attack. And this particular heart attack is called the widow-maker because in 80 percent of the cases of a hundred percentage blockage, the patient always dies." And he goes, "You're going to be in the 20 percent 'cause I'm good at my job." And he disappears into my crotch, punched a hole into my groin, fed a tube into my heart through my femoral, and stuck a stent into that LAD and opened it up. So the dude saved my life.

But before he did that, I was laying on the table after he told me 80/20. So either you go, "Man, I have a 20 percent chance of living" or you're like, "Man, I have an 80 percent chance of dying right now. Either way, it's kinda fuckin' bad odds and shit." So I was sitting there going, "This might be it." More so than any other moment in my life, where I'd potentially gotten hit by a fuckin' bus, I might fuckin' die tonight. This could be the end and I'm forty-seven. And I was like, "Well I'm lying on the table and I can't do anything and they've got me hopped up on fuckin' drugs and shit."

So I'm like, "How do you feel? You spent your whole life fuckin' with your head up your ass, looking at your head and heart, so what do you fuckin' think about all this?" And I was okay with where I was. I had a good life. I had a good run. Everything worked out for me and shit like that. And I got to live a life that I didn't think I was ever going to lead. Great parents, great brother and sister, and wonderful friends, and great wife and fantastic kid, and my career was my own. It was my own unique thing. Like, fuckin' you can't duplicate it and shit. It wasn't generic. It was very uniquely mine." So it was like, "You did it. Fuckin' push away from the table. If this is it, take it gracefully. If you're done, just don't be the last guy at the party fuckin' hangin' out, being like, 'Hey, man, you got any donuts?'" Just fuckin' get out. Time to go. Be appreciative. Be grateful. Move the fuck on. And I was. I've reached a place of peace. If it fuckin' goes, it goes and shit.

But I did say to myself, "Reboot." I said that was my only regret. I was like, "Fuck, I wish we had gotten to make Jay and Silent Bob Reboot," 'cause I knew what the script was, and I felt like, "Ah, it would have been fun." That's the only regret I had about potentially dying and partially tied to the fact that I was like, "If I do die tonight, then Yoga Hosers was the last movie I ever made. Fuck, I wish I had gone out on Jay and Silent Bob Reboot."

So after I survived the heart attack, I was like, "Fuck. We're definitely making this movie." And the movie was the post–heart attack movie. It acts as this—not last will and testament, but a final statement summation on not just my movie career but podcasting stuff and my personal life. 'Cause I was like, "If you get one heart attack, potentially you can have more." So I was like, "If it fuckin' comes back—my father had two—and takes me next time, I've got to leave something out there that says a bit more about me. And also it was the twenty-fifth anniversary of Clerks this year, so it felt like this was the time to make a movie that's funny, but looked back.

Jason and Kevin get emotional at the wrap of
*Jay and Silent Bob Reboot*, 2019.

**KEVIN SMITH**

**Kevin Smith:** So we made the flick. It was a little weird. I thought it would be easy as fuck to do. It was actually kind of one of the harder flicks I've made in my life. We didn't have enough time or money. It was like stuffing twenty pounds of shit in a ten-pound bag, and that's I'm sure what the critics will say about it. But it was a lot more work. And Jordan [Monsanto], who's the producer, and Liz [Destro, producer], tried to explain that going in. I was like, "We got $10 million to make the movie. Thank God."

And they're like, "That's not nearly enough."

And again, the schedule called for thirty-five days. We dropped it down to twenty-five and eventually got to twenty-one. So when you lose days, you lose money. And the reason those days all existed was to make it a shoot that wouldn't exhaust anybody, or anything like that.

But at the end of the day, in order to make the movie, you had to really work. And generally, you'd like it to be just fun and shit. It was fun, but at the same time, I slept about four hours a night. Believe me, I was happy 'cause all my dreams were coming true.

But you'd shoot for twelve to fifteen hours a day. I would edit until I fell asleep. Sleep for four hours, get up and start again. It was just like making *Clerks*. And we had the same amount of days. *Clerks* was shot over the course of twenty-one days, but with no days off. This was shot in twenty-one days, but we had weekends off. So, yeah, it was crazily similar. But the difference being that *Clerks* was $27,000 and this was $10 million. But we needed more. It was a $20 million movie. That was the only bridge. And that's what I'd say to myself. Any time a problem presented itself or there's a budgetary thing, we had to lose something or whatever, I would be like, "This is the bridge we have to cross to make *Reboot*. This is it. It ain't gonna be easy, but it'll be gratifying. And if I really want to do it, we'll cross those bridges." And we did! So it took a minute or two to reorganize the head space.

But man oh man, Harley made it wonderful, as did Jason. Jason was fantastic. The first day he was really rusty and it was worrisome. And first day was with Jason Lee, and it was like ten pages of dialogue in the mall, all the expository shit, setting up the whole movie and whatnot. And Jason Lee hadn't acted in four years, but he hit the ground running. Fuck, he was Brodie again. And he had all the mouthsful, big speeches, and he was crushing it.

Jay came to set a little bit overconfident, like I did. How I came to set going, "I know how to direct. I've been fuckin' doing this twenty-five years. I do it for CW." He, too, came to the set a little too confident. He didn't learn all his lines in advance. Jay is used to acting for the last fuckin' ten to fifteen years. He gets smaller parts on things. So you could show up on a set; they give you your sides for the scene you're shooting that day. And while you're in the make-up chair, you can memorize your sides. That's how he's been used to working for the last decade. However, he forgot that you can't possibly do that on a Kevin Smith movie. There's just too much fucking dialogue to sit there and get it in the chair. You'll be fucked and you'll stick out like a sore thumb. And he did.

Jason Lee memorized the shit out of the dialogue we'd rehearsed with him the night before. And Jason Mewes didn't and therefore didn't know everything. So as we shot, it became apparent. What was scheduled to be a twelve-hour day—and easily could have been an eight-hour day 'cause it was three old friends walking around a room and talking, no special effects, no dinosaurs, nothing like that—became a fifteen-hour day on day one. We went over schedule. And that was terrifying. So I was like, "Oh my God." I had a heart-to-heart with him. I was like, "I worked too hard to get here. I did not know you would be the bullet. I'm always looking over my shoulders where the bullet's coming from. It can't be you. You're the other guy in the movie. Your name's in the fuckin' title!" That was only day one.

Day two onward, he was absolutely stellar. And I didn't have to really even beat him up about it. He beat himself up, because that fifteen hours, it was all him. Every time we had to do another take, clearly it was him. So you feel that over the day. You start [going], like, "Oh my God. We're going again because of me." You carry it like a fuckin' cross. So he self-corrected extraordinarily. The next day, a hundred eighty fuckin' degrees in the other direction. He knew [everyone's] dialogue.

There was a guy named Dom, a friend of his, Dominic [Burns], who was a producer on the movie that Jason had directed called *Madness in the Method*. I guess he wrote the story. He had done that a couple of months before he went to do *Reboot*. So Dom was there with us 'cause he was a big Jay and Silent Bob fan, 'cause he just wanted to watch. But Dom became Jason's touchstone. Every night, Jason and Dom would run lines. And when Jason wasn't on camera, he was running lines with Dom. Dom was his real-life Silent Bob. While I was off making the movie, Jason was constantly running lines with Dom. Dom was an absolute lifesaver. And Jason was golden. He's so fuckin' fantastic in the movie. He gets emotional and cries in the movie. He makes you cry 'cause you've known this character for twenty-five years, and he ain't about tears. But when he gets emotional, you can't help get emotional. So he delivered a career-best performance, easily. And the emotional stuff had everything to do with Harley playing his daughter. So my daughter played his daughter. Because if my daughter plays my daughter, that's not acting, that's real life. But if she plays his daughter, that's fuckin' a performance.

She has known Jason since she came out the womb. She had this pink elephant she carried around forever, [that] she still has in her room, which she called "YayYay." That was her childhood fuckin' snuggie comfort blanket. That was her trying to say "Jay." So she loved this fuckin' dude from the moment she popped out, and he's loved her even more so 'cause he's always wanted to be a dad. He'd always say it. Then he had Logan, his daughter. And you realized he's an amazing fuckin' father. He didn't know his dad, so that made him an amazing dad to somebody else. It made him want to overdeliver for his kid, be

the dad that he never had. So, him acting with Harley, when her character Millie got emotional, Jay responded to that.

Harley's a pretty wonderful actress at this point, and she can cry on cue and stuff. She went to Stella Adler "method," learned to be an actress. Jason never did any training, so if we had him standing opposite another actress, and she was crying about being his daughter, I think Jason would have done a fine job, but he wouldn't have cried. But to have Harley standing opposite him, crying during her performance, he just fuckin' broke down too. So suddenly you get an elevated peak. You get something out of a guy you never in a million years thought you'd get. This secret weapon of the funniest person you know suddenly going glassy-eyed because his heart's broken. Oh, it's fuckin' magnifique!

Everyone coming to that movie, they will expect to laugh, right? In the sequel to *Jay and Silent Bob Strike Back*, fuckin' Jay and Silent Bob better be in it, and we better fuckin' laugh. They'll get that. But what they're gonna get, which they're not counting on, is the beating heart, man. And that was because it was a post-heart-attack movie. I just couldn't make a bunch of jokes. I had to say something a little more meaningful, something a little more heartfelt. And him having a kid for the last four years absolutely informed it. And me, watching him be an incredible dad, almost wishing that he had gone before me and had a kid before I had a kid, because I would have learned how to be a better dad from watching him go ahead of me. I said, "That's the movie. The guy least likely." None of us thought that Jason would be a good dad, and he's the best dad in the world. So what if Jay, his character, had a kid, you know? And boom, there we went.

**David Gati:** Wow! That's great. Yeah.

Jason and daughter Logan, 2017
*Courtesy of Jordan Monsanto*

Joshua Buchanan | Howell, Missouri |
"Jay," 2015

# "THIS IS FOR THE FUCKIN' FANS"

**Kevin Smith:** [Fans], I love 'em. Honestly, that's why I did it. I get approached by folks in public a lot. I've been doing this for the past twenty-five years. But I would say over the course of the last ten years, not just "Oh, you look like Silent Bob," they're like, "Oh, you're Kevin Smith." I started as director Kevin Smith, and then probably twelve years into my career, maybe it begins when we do the *Eventings with Kevin Smith* DVDs, but I start being "Kevin Smith" for a living. So that becomes your job 24/7, and it never ends. When you're a director, your job ends when the movie's finished. And you can take time off and then go make another movie if you want, and generally you want to.

If you are yourself for a living, the job never fuckin' ends unless you go to sleep, and even then the job's going on behind your back. And then you wake up. It's about job maintenance. It's about vying for a little bit of attention in a world where everybody's paying to get that attention. And they're also selling way more cool wares than I am. You know, "Watch these motherfuckin' superheroes take down the building. Watch these fuckin' dinosaurs eat a shark and shit." My shingle is like, "My characters talk about those movies!? And we've been here for a quarter century." That's it.

I do my own thing; that's what I'm known for. So if you like that, come over here. And that's a huge testimony to the fact that I've been able to do it for a quarter of a century. That has everything to do with the audience. EVERYTHING! We don't get to make *Reboot* unless there's an audience. Unless I can count on repaying my equity investors on the movie, by going on tour with the movie. That's all audience-based; that's faith in the fandom, faith in the folks who are like, "Oh my God, I wish you'd make another movie about Jay and Silent Bob."

I feel like I've met every fan face-to-face 'cause I do a lot of cons. I do a lot of live podcasts. But then you put it into action, with them as an integral part of it. It wasn't made in a vacuum. A lot of filmmakers get to make their movies in a vacuum. They don't think about the audience. Fuck, they don't want to be thinking about the audience. They couldn't be fucked to think about the audience 'cause to them, they're like, "Well, that would fuck with my vision." Or I've seen some creative people be like, "The audience don't know what they want until I give it to them." I could never feel that way about my shit. Way too appreciative of anyone showing up, 'cause I've done things where people showed up and I've done things where nobody fuckin' showed up. But I've been around a quarter century and that's all because of the audience. What keeps me going, why I get to make [*Reboot*], is because people go, "But he does have that audience. They'll pay. Somebody's gonna show up. They'll fuckin' fuel it."

Thankfully, they didn't do the math and be like, "Well, they didn't show up for *Yoga Hosers*." But [film executives] were like, "I think they'll show up for *Jay and Silent Bob* [*Reboot*]." So then you just design the thing to be fool-proof based on the audience, knowing that we go out on tour and me and Jay sit next to each other with no movie, and just talk to each other as *Jay and Silent Bob Get Old*, and the audience will fuckin' shell out forty to seventy-five bucks. It's amazing! So I'm like, "What if we went back and gave 'em a fuckin' movie that they've been asking us to make for the last twenty years? They'd probably pay the same fuckin' price and have a great fuckin' time. We can only make those decisions based on the audience, man. So I've spent a long time with the audience, interacting with them, going way back to the beginning.

# SHRINE TO CLERKS

**Kevin Smith:** Ming Chen had made this *Clerks* shrine. I had to go to the Internet Café in Redbank 'cause I didn't even have a fuckin' computer to go look at something. My girlfriend, she was in college, so she had access to the Internet. She said, "I saw this beautiful website, this shrine to *Clerks*."

I said, "What's a website?"

She told me, "Go look at the Internet Café."

So I paid five bucks, got online, and the guy showed me . . . it wasn't Google, I guess fuckin' Yahoo or Jeeves or whatever the fuck to find this website made by this guy Ming Chen, who was a student going to school in Michigan, at U Mich, I think. And so he liked *Clerks* a lot and he built this website. And I didn't even have the terminology to describe it. This is how I described the website, first time I saw it, "It's like a magazine but on a television." That's what it felt like. Like, "Oh my God, there's graphics and there's a story and you turn pages, but there's no paper. It's fuckin' fascinating!" So from that point forward, I was kind of involved with the audience.

I reached out to the guy who built the website, Ming Chen, and was like, "Hey, man. Can you build a website for me?"

And he was like, "Yeah, what do you want me to do?"

I was like, "I want to do a website for View Askew Productions. We made *Clerks*. Obviously you like *Clerks*. We got this movie *Mallrats* coming out and stuff."

So Ming started building the View Askew website, viewaskew.com. As we went through it, I gave him pictures, wrote things for all the pictures and shit like that—curated it, as they would say now. But then, at the end of it, right before he took it public, I said, "I want to do this thing where once a week we do a town hall 'cause I like doing Q&A live. Is there a way to do video Q&A?"

He said, "Uh, it might take a minute." He's going, "But what we could do, we could put up a white board."

I said, "What's that?"

He said, "It's just a message board. A bunch of people post messages and then you answer them whenever you want to. You don't have to get to it right away. You can do it at two, three in the morning."

And I was like, "That sounds fuckin' interesting. All right, man, yeah, do that. Do a message board. I can interact with people? People that actually bought fuckin' tickets?" 'Cause I didn't know the audience part of that. All I knew was audience data. Like, you sold this many tickets. Or critics—they represented the audience 'cause they wrote about the movie. But it wasn't democratized yet. It wasn't like anybody could jump online and be like, "This is what I thought of fuckin' *Jaws*."

So, you know, for me, I was like, "Let's do it. Let's do this message board." He puts it up. It goes live, and I realized I would never be alone again. It could be five in the morning and I'd wake up, fuckin' go to the message board, and answer questions people left me, Easter eggs in the night. They wanted information only I could provide, so I felt necessary and useful.

# IT'S THE MOVIE BUSINESS

**Kevin Smith:** We never thought 'bout selling 'em anything. I remember somebody asking me on the message board, "What are you selling?"

And I was like, "I don't know. The movies, I guess. The idea of these movies. What would we be selling?"

"Don't you have T-shirts or posters or anything like that?"

Never occurred to me to sell that shit. Never occurred to me [that] people would want that shit. As a kid who grew up with *Star Wars* toys, you'd imagine I was ready for that shit. But I'm like, "Who would want fuckin' T-shirts of this black-and-white movie? Who would want fuckin' action figures of these movies?" I found we had a closet full of *Mallrats* posters that Universal had given us. And *Mallrats* tanked and went away so fast, and they were in the fuckin' closet 'cause nobody wanted them. And then I was like, "Well, I guess I've got *Mallrats* posters. I can sign 'em if you want those. Fuck yeah." So I think I started signing 'em, and we started selling them for ten or twenty bucks through mail order with SASE, self-addressed stamped envelope; you send a check or money order. Sometimes there were phone orders, but there was no Internet business at that point for us. That came later on.

So the site got built by the fans. My business got built by the fans. I sell merchandise all the time. I sell T-shirts. I sell toys. I sell sculptures. All the dopey shit that I've created only because the fans asked for it and said, "Here's an idea." And I still do it to this day. All the crap or ephemera that exists in the world that has my face or my friends' faces on it or looks like us or fuckin' voodoo dolls of us or whatever—that's because the audience willed it into existence, not me. It was a great fuckin' ego-feed for me, where I was like, "You want to buy a toy of me? Let's make that happen. They want a toy of me!" I'll go to hell for the amount of fuckin' plastic I've put into the world, I'm sure. Once I get to the other side, Jesus will be like, "It's all about plastic. Didn't you watch *The Graduate*?" And send me straight to hell. But in this world, I got to make a bunch of cool toys and shit because of the fans.

Everything I've got to do is because of the fans. And I've heard some people say, when they accept an award, like, "This is for the fuckin' fans" and shit. I don't mean it like that. I mean literally: if I have no fans, I don't get to keep going. Like, you know, *Clerks* is a magic trick, so maybe you get people to "Gather round. Watch this!" like once. You know, *Mallrats* didn't work at all until fuckin' years later. What a slow burn that was. What a late bloomer. You know, *Chasing Amy* . . . right on time, the work of somebody who's like, "I think I got the hang of this right now." But I don't get to *Chasing Amy* 'cause *Mallrats* was such a fuckin' disaster without fans. People are like, "I like that *Clerks* movie." And even the few that fuckin' paid to go see *Mallrats* in the theater were like, "I recognize myself in those characters." Like, "I am Brodie. My God, I collect comic books too and shit." They stuck around. It wasn't enough to make Universal happy, make a bunch of money. [*Mallrats*] cost $5 million to make and we only made $2 million at the box office. But when it got to home video, they made a lot of money and I made a lot of fans

Designing the View Askew website, 1996

The logo for the Secret Stash,
where Kevin sells his merch

'cause people finally saw the movie and [were] like, "That's me." They didn't get to see it in the theater. They saw it at home. So fans built my career. Back in the day, they didn't give a fuck about my box office, not the fans, the people I worked for. The people who gave me millions of dollars to make my art were easy on me about my box office because my home video was incredibly strong.

**David Gati:** Oh yeah.

**KS:** And that was because of the fans. And they always knew, everything I've gotten to do, past fuckin' 1997-98, generally has the fans attached to it. Or any business decision that goes in my favor is generally because people are like, "Why the fuck is he still here? He's been doin' this twenty-five years with varying degrees of success, but he's still fuckin' here and he ain't Chris Nolan. Like, he's got a reason to be here, old Chris Nolan. He ain't fuckin' Judd Apatow. He had a string of successes. Why is this fucker still here?" And it's because I've got the fan base. I've got a bunch of people who would fuckin' shell out money. They'll wait in line for hours to tell me this profoundly moving story about how some bullshit I made up years ago affected and/or saved their lives. You know how fuckin' impactful that is?

Don't get me wrong. I'm a capitalist. I like the money. I like the money that comes with the movie business. This is a nice house. But I don't do it for the money, and that's good, 'cause I don't make all the money. This is also a very deceptive house. But that being said, I had to let go of the notion of doing it for money like way fuckin' early on, when I realized I didn't have mainstream ideas. I just wanted to make Kevin Smith movies. And they're in good for a lot of fuckin' money. They're good for enough but not a fuck-ton, and people are in the fuck-ton business. In the '90s, you could squeak by with respectability and shit. The indie-film movement was more about "We're doing it!" rather than "What's it making?" and shit like that. So business eventually catches up.

**Kevin Smith:** By the time I'd stopped making expensive movies, the highest-budgeted movie I've ever made was Cop Out—$30 million, but we came in under budget, like $26 million. Now, I don't know who would give me $30 million for one of my ideas. Nobody ever! And to be fair, I never got $30 million for one of my ideas, but somebody gave me $20 million to make Jay and Silent Bob Strike Back. That's confounding! Wow! What the fuck?! For two-bit characters in the background of your fuckin' other movies? And we couldn't expect that that would repeat in this fuckin' day and age. So one could make the argument, I've been around twenty-five years, that I'm not in the ascendant stage of my career, I must be on the descendent stage of my career.

Without the fan base, I wouldn't have a career. I'd be done. I'd be waxing nostalgic, as I do often. Believe me, I say Clerks more than anybody that has ever said Clerks in the entire history of mankind. And I say it like nineteen, twenty-eight times a day. That all being said, it's because of them [that] I got to keep going. I should have been done a long fucking time ago. By conventional business standards, I should have been out on my ass post-Mallrats. Luckily, I was shrewd on Chasing Amy. I kept my budget low and did something that fuckin' connected. But Dogma cost $10 million, makes $30 [million], but that's not sexy. That's not going to make anyone drop their drawers or take their fuckin' top off. It's like, "Oh, that's respectable," especially for a weird movie like that. You know, for a minute, I have this cool little corner of R-rated comedies that didn't have to make too much money.

Then Judd Apatow came along and was like, "These movies can make a hundred million dollars if you do 'em right." So at that point, suddenly I was like, "Oh shit, I should redefine what I do. Other people are doing what I do and doing it better and making more money at it." But that's when I faced, "Well, you were never in it for the money." There was never any dream about, like, "I'll make the big movie one day." The only dream was Clerks. I just wanted to make Clerks. I just wanted to see what it looked like. I wanted to make the movie. I worked in a convenience store. Nobody had made a convenience-store movie yet. It seemed like a good idea. It just seemed like a magic trick. It seemed clever. It never felt brilliant. It never felt smart. It never felt genius. It never felt like the voice of a generation. Felt clever. If I'm guilty of anything, it's of feeling clever my entire life. Anything that works . . . I'm like, "Fuck, that was clever!" I don't think it's talent. I don't think it's genius. I don't think it's like, "Look at that. It's a fuckin' classic. It will stand the test of time." I don't think I need it to stand the test of time. I think I need this shit to just stay in my lifetime. So when I'm done, what do I give a fuck? If it keeps going on, that's up to my kid. If she's a good kid, she'll keep people talking about *Clerks*. She'll take over saying *Clerks* nineteen, twenty-eight times a day.

Framed picture of Kevin at his home, surrounded by his favorites
*Courtesy of Sally Gati*

# SPINNING PLATES

**Kevin Smith:** I just want to go to my grave doing the same shit I've been doing since I was twenty-two, since fuckin' *Clerks* happened to me. I think there's a way to do it. You just don't grab for everything. You know, be content with who likes you. And with every new project, perhaps you add to it, and every new project ain't just a film. Sometimes it's a podcast. Sometimes you've got people who are in your audience because they've watched you in an episode of fuckin' *Degrassi*.

I've spun a lot of plates, and there's a long tail behind me of things that I've done that's not the one thing that I started doing. And I do that for self-preservation. If I was just a director, I'd been done a long fuckin' time ago. Because I'm Kevin Smith professionally, and there's only one fuckin' person that can fire me. And I'm very happy with Kevin Smith's performance, so I'm going to keep him employed. That and death, and they came close. But until they fuckin' win, I'm gonna keep doing that, but that's only because of the fan base.

I'm always telling people, "Take your movie on the road, like I did." And they're like, "Bro, I don't have a fan base like you."

And I know that's the perception from the outside too. People are like, "Jesus, he gets to do so fuckin' much because he has an audience that fuckin' goes with him. He's like the Grateful Dead or fuckin' Phish. There ain't enough to fuckin' pop him onto the Top 10 chart, but apparently you don't need that to live pretty fuckin' well."

As long as you don't have the big stuff, which I don't anymore. But yeah . . . the fans are everything, and I don't mean that in a kind of like, "Oh, I love my fans. The fans are everything." They are the life blood of what I do. I get to do this for as long as they're interested. So, ultimately, I'm not the boss. I'm not the only one. They are. Once the audience loses interest in me altogether, once I can't put together 200 people in a room, 50 people in a room—you know, fuckin' a few responses on Twitter, fuckin' any likes on Instagram and shit like that—then I'll know that, like, "All right, there's nothing left—I'm finished. The audience is kind of done with me or I've outlived the audience.

They've all fuckin' died." And that's probably gonna be the likely case. At that point, I'll push back.

But they're still there, and there's all different shit . . . Some people don't know the movies at all. They're like, "Oh my God, I loved *Comic Book Men*, you and your friends."

"Did you see the movies?"

"You had movies? You made a *Comic Book Men* movie?"

"No. Before that show, I made a bunch of movies. We talked about that the whole time."

"I never knew what that was."

Some cats know me from, like, "You were on *Degrassi*." Some people just know me as a podcaster. Some people know me as a fuckin' *Talking Dead* guest. I'll be out in public and people will be like, "You're the best guest on *Talking Dead*." They don't know anything else I fuckin' do. Like, "I don't know what you do, bro, but I fuckin' love you on *Talking Dead*. You always say the right shit."

I spin a lot of plates for that very reason, so that if one of those plates stops or somebody's like, "You're not allowed to do this anymore," I can just pivot over to here. But all that requires an audience, and I got to do all that shit because of the audience.

So the AUDIENCE, as you asked, is EVERYTHING.

Kevin and Jason with fans Matt Westphalen and his kids, 2016
*Courtesy of Matt Westphalen*

"We helped set the Guinness World Record for most
Jay & Silent Bob cosplayers."—Ryan James, 2017
*Courtesy of Red Bank Pulse*

**KEVIN SMITH**

Guinness World Record turnout for Jay & Silent Bob cosplay, 2017
*Courtesy of Red Bank Pulse*

# CLERKS III

2022

# FRIENDSHIP

**WHILE WORKING ON THE SCRIPT** for *Clerks III*, Kevin Smith shot his fourteenth film, *Killroy Was Here*, a horror comedy anthology. Made with students from Ringling College of Art and Design in Florida, the film is about a monster based on a World War II graffiti meme. In 2022, Legendao minted nonfungible tokens for this film, the very first feature released as an NFT.

After a few different incarnations of the *Clerks III* script, plus a reunion with Jeff Anderson, Kevin finally brought his old friends back from the dead. With the original cast members, it was now possible to make his fifteenth film. He resuscitated the characters that had started the whole shebang and returned to the original site from where everything was born.

Within the context of Kevin's fans, it would be anticlimactic to say that his fans weren't waiting for this, for this was their Holy Grail. There will always be some people out there on the Internet who posit that Kevin was a "one-hit wonder," and here he was, reaching back to the well one more time. But his true fans knew that this film was a kind of redemption, a way to finish a story. As with all his movies, Kevin had a way to make them personal and to speak to exactly where he was at the time. He used his own life: surviving a heart attack and getting healthy; mending his relationships; trying, failing, and succeeding. Kevin was just like his fans, and they were there for him. Ultimately, it was about getting to be around the people who had supported him from the very beginning.

# REUNITING WITH JEFF ANDERSON

ON OCTOBER 1, 2019, KEVIN WROTE ON INSTAGRAM THAT HE HAD MET UP WITH JEFF ANDERSON AND TALKED TO HIM ABOUT GETTING THE ORIGINAL GROUP MEMBERS BACK TOGETHER. IT WAS HIS CHANCE TO TAKE EVERYTHING HE HAD BEEN THROUGH AND PUT IT INTO A FILM ABOUT HIS JOURNEY FROM THE CONVENIENCE STORE AND BACK AGAIN.

"3 CLERKS! Thanks to the good folks at Leeloo Multiprops, I got to see Randal! Jeff Anderson, Jason Mewes, and I spent Saturday signing stuff and catching up, seeing so much movie merch that's been made over the last 25 years (hit the Leloo site for sweet signed skateboards)! But even better than that? We talked about making a movie together. It'll be a movie that concludes a saga. It'll be a movie about how you're never too old to completely change your life. It'll be a movie about how a decades-spanning friendship finally confronts the future. It'll be a movie that brings us back to the beginning - a return to the cradle of civilization in the great state of New Jersey. It'll be a movie that stars Jeff and @briancohalloran, with me and Jay in supporting roles. And it'll be a movie called *CLERKS III*!"

# FINAL SCRIPT

IN AN INSTAGRAM POST FROM JANUARY 14, 2021, KEVIN WROTE ABOUT FINISHING THE SCRIPT, WHICH TAKES PLACE IN THE CONVENIENCE STORE. AFTER RANDAL SURVIVES A MASSIVE HEART ATTACK, HE DECIDES TO MAKE A MOVIE ABOUT HIS LIFE AT QUICK STOP WITH HIS FRIENDS DANTE, ELIAS, JAY, AND SILENT BOB.

I started writing CLERKS III on December 28th and just finished the 101 page first draft last night! But the writing doesn't begin when you start tapping the keys: I've been stirring this stew in my brain pan for awhile now. So when I sat down to put years of daydreaming into actual words, the typing part of the writing process was pretty brisk. Fake New Jersey (or what I've long called the View Askewniverse) has been so much more preferable to visit than the real world lately - but I've told the tale I wanted to tell, so it's time to step back, hand the script off to a trusted few, and then tinker further based on the feedback. For those keeping score anymore, this is actually Clerks III v.2. I had written a different version of Clerks III about 6 years back - one which I'm now very happy we never made (although I used the opening scene for @jayandsilentbob Reboot). This is a much more personal story than the previous incarnation, drawing directly on the heart attack that nearly killed me (3 years ago next month). It was oddly triggering writing those scenes, as it was the first time in awhile I contemplated how close I came to shuffling lose this mortal coil. But far more than make me mindful of my own mortality, this script to Clerks III makes me laugh out loud. Dante, Randal, Elias, Becky, Jay and Silent Bob are all back, and the premise of the flick allows anyone who was in Clerks or Clerks II to return in some capacity. After a bummer of a 2020, this is how I want to spend some of 2021: at @quickstopgroceries in New Jersey where it all began, with friends and family. And when we finally roll cameras on Clerks III, I will know beyond the shadow of a doubt that I *am* supposed to be there that day! #KevinSmith #clerks3 #clerks #clerks2

*Above:* In this Instagram post from August 26, 2021, three days before the end of the *Clerks III* shoot, Kevin is at the monitor showing an image from the original film, with Dante and Randal in the same spot at Quick Stop: "It's been a blissful trip to the past in the Wayback Machine. Took 7 years to get here and now it's almost over."

*Right:* PL Boucher | Montreal, Canada | "*Clerks III* Teaser," 2015

**KEVIN SMITH**

A fan movie poster that revisits Quick Stop. In *Clerks III*, Kevin re-created events from the original film, bringing it up-to-date.

Tim Doyle | Austin, Texas | "*Clerks* screening poster," 2011

# EPILOGUE

Nathan Thomas Miliner | Louisville, Kentucky |
"SMITH," 2010.

# HERE'S LOOKIN' AT YOU, KEV!

"**SEEING** *CLERKS* at the Vogue my freshman year in college was like a freaking rock concert and I was instantly a fan, from the very beginning of the View Askew arrival. Here is writer/director Kevin Smith along with characters from his films, from top to bottom: Jeff Anderson and Brian O'Halloran in *Clerks*, Jason Lee in *Mallrats*, Joey Lauren Adams and Ben Affleck in *Chasing Amy*, Chris Rock in *Dogma*, Jason Mewes and Kevin Smith in *Jay & Silent Bob Strike Back*, Rosario Dawson in *Clerks 2*, Elizabeth Banks, Justin Long and Seth Rogen in *Zack and Miri Make a Porno*."

–Nathan Thomas Milliner

Logan Pack | Roswell, New Mexico | "Jay and Silent Bob Get Super Powers!" 2012

Jordan Howard | Southampton, United Kingdom | "Jay & Silent Bob," 2014

Jordan Howard | Southampton, United Kingdom | "Jay & Silent Bob (Splatter)," 2012

KEVIN SMITH

Ben "Steamroller" Steeves | Toronto,
Canada | "Stoner-boy and Lunchbox,"
2005

Brandon Sparks | Little Elm, Texas |
"Jay & Silent Bob Calaveras (circa *Clerks*)," 2014

Blake Stevenson | Ontario, Canada |
"Jay and Silent Bob: Clerks," 2009

Mural of Jay and Silent Bob
in Seminyak, Bali, Indonesia
*Courtesy of Kimia Shariat*

Mural of Jay and Silent Bob
outside Donnie Mac's Trailer Park
Cuisine in Boise, Idaho, 2011
*Courtesy of Chad Estes*

**KEVIN SMITH**

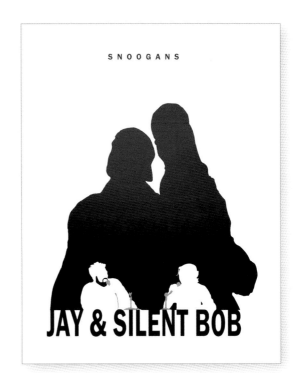

Steve Garcia | Middletown,
New Jersey | "Snoogans"

Adam Hicks | Indiana | "Half Half Whole,"
2009

Carlos Duplessis | Texas | "Jay & Silent Bob," 2011

*Above:* Meto Cross | Rostov-on-Don, Russia | "Jay & Silent Bob," 2015

*Right:* Nikolett Mikula | Szigetszentmiklós, Hungary | "Minimal Style – Jay and Silent Bob," 2015

KEVIN SMITH

Martín Laksman | Buenos Aires, Argentina | "Jay and Silent Bob," 2011

Quintin Navales Jr. | Modesto, California |
"Bluntman & Chronic," 2008

Phil Cho | Columbia, Maryland |
"Bluntman & Chronic," 2012
(inspired by one of Jim Lee's
*All Star* designs)

Luis Giuliani | Vancouver, British
Columbia | "Kevin Smith directing
an episode of *The Flash*," 2016

Flew to Vancouver to direct my third ep of
@TheCWSupergirl
& @MelissaBenoist was on my flight! I was a
l'il disappointed she needed a plane.

12:29 AM - 14 Aug 2017

Kevin with Melissa Benoist, taking a break from
directing *Supergirl*, 2017
*Courtesy of Warner Bros. Television*

Shawn Surface | Orlando, Florida |
"Boys Night Out," 2007
(based on characters owned by DC,
Marvel, and Kevin Smith)

# LOOKING BACK

**Kevin Smith:** It took me twenty years to become something of an acceptable, passable filmmaker. I know what to do with the camera now, but that's not how I got into it. I didn't get into it to show off the pictures. I saw *Slacker* and I said, "This is funny. People think this is funny. I can do funny. And if this counts as funny, it's just dudes sitting around in Texas. I could do dudes sitting around in New Jersey." So what I learned was it doesn't matter what it looks like as long as they're with the content, as long as you're saying something they haven't heard before or at least saying something remotely interesting to them. And they let me ride on the *Clerks* flick big-time on the look, so much so that for the next ten years, I never put any effort into making a better-looking film. It would happen regardless around me, with more money and better, different DPs. Like Dave Klein, who I shot with first, knew as much as me. He'd get better over the years, and suddenly the shit would start looking better too. But for me, that was never the game.

And so, whenever people ask me, "Is it important for a film to look good?," in my opinion, absolutely not. It could look as bad as *Clerks*, as long as what you're saying inside or what you're showing is something new, or at least a spin on something familiar that's a fresh perspective. First film, they'll let you go. By the time I was on my third or fourth film, that's when they started going, "Is this guy gonna move the camera around? He does not know what he's doing with a fucking camera." And I would always be like, "Yeah, that don't matter because nobody cares as long as the content's there, as long as the message is cool, as long as the characters are cool." So when you hear the answer from me, going, like, "Don't worry about the look"—remember, take it with a grain of salt because I was never the "look" guy.

And now we're in a world where there are far more people jockeying for these positions, far more people trying to get through the gate, not even fill a position here in Hollywood, [but] make their own shit. The equipment is such that filmmaking is completely democratized. It used to be you had to have some money to do it. Now you can shoot it on a fuckin' iPhone, cut it on an iPhone, upload it to YouTube. We can all make films. When you're trying to do something as personal as write and direct a film, it's like writing a poem to someone. And rather than just one person, it's going to the world. It's gotta be as much of you as possible. When you're writing/directing, man, that's coming out of you. It's a piece of your soul that you're ploppin' on a platter and putting up for people to see. I would, if I had to do it over again, I'd probably do it the same way.

Keelan Ashton-Bell (aka Killustrate) | Melbourne, Australia | "A Night with Kevin Smith," 2012

Upper Deck Skybox *Clerks* Trading Card, 2017
*Courtesy of Check Out My Collectibles*

"Live a 'why not?' life, man.

Take the shot. The shot is always worth taking."

– Kevin Smith

# ENDNOTES

# THANK-YOUS

To Kevin Smith, the source and inspiration for everything in this book—for his stories, personal photos, and words of encouragement.
Forever grateful!

To my mom, who believed it was possible, sometimes even more than I did.

Big thanks to all the talented fan artists, photographers, and reviewers who contributed to this book.

Thanks to these websites for sharing their photos and content:

deviantart.com

facebook.com/yesthatkevinsmith

fuckyeahjasonmewes.tumblr.com

instagram.com/thatkevinsmith

jayandsilentbob.com

silentbobspeaks.com

smodcast.com

thisisnotporn.net

twitter.com/jenschwalbach

twitter.com/thatkevinsmith

viewaskew.com

# CREDITS

*SModcast* 259 (podcast), "The Walrus and the Carpenter,"
June 25, 2013
*TUSK* ORIGIN, 125-127

*SModcast* 285 (podcast), "Sundance 94, Pt. 1,"
January 22, 2014
JIM JACKS, 44

*SModcast* 286 (podcast), "Sundance 94 Pt. 2,"
January 29, 2014
DAVE KEHR REVIEW, 34
KEEPING HOPE ALIVE, 34
NEWS FROM THE FRONT LINES, 34

*SModcast* 306 (podcast), "The Darrin Diaries,"
September 2, 2014
WORKING WITH HARLEY, 133

*SModcast* 312 (podcast), "Randal Reflects,"
October 28, 2014
JOHN PIERSON, 31
SUBMITTING TO SUNDANCE, 33

*SModcast* 337 (podcast), "The Bad News Bear,"
October 20, 2015
INDEPENDENT FEATURE FILM MARKET, 28-29

*SModcast* 345 (podcast), "A Letter from 1984,"
January 13, 2016
VILMOS AND RATFACE, 82

*SModcast* 368 (podcast), "Rebootch to the Nootch,"
February 14, 2017
MY BIGGEST FAN, 76

*SModcast* 420 (podcast), "Kevin Smith Reboots Hall-H,"
July 24, 2019
BEN'S BACK, 151-154

*SMovieMakers* 12 (podcast), "Vincent Pereira—The Lynch Pin,
Pt. 2," September 26, 2012
FILM SCHOOL, 18
FIRST VERSION OF THE SCRIPT, 19
MEET JEFF ANDERSON, 20
*SLACKER*, 17

*Snowball Effect: The Story of "Clerks"* (documentary), 2004
BOB HAWK/PETER BRODERICK/AMY TAUBIN, 30
FINAL SUNDANCE SCREENING, 35-37
HARVEY WALKS OUT, 32
HOW TO PAY FOR IT, 23
PRODUCTION, 26
REPPING THE FILM, 31
THE ENDING, 32
WRAPPING UP, 27

*Spoilers with Kevin Smith* (TV show), "Gore Score and
Severed Ears Ago," June 25, 2012
JASON LEE, 46

# CONTRIBUTORS INDEX

# FAN TESTIMONIALS

Kevin Smith is an anomaly - both an iconic filmmaker and an enormous fan of films and entertainment himself. And that makes me a huge fan of his. He is so confident yet so humble at the same time, and he dove into podcasting like a great explorer. Having my podcast on his network all these years and getting to act in some of his projects have been some of the biggest highlights of my life.

— Ben Gleib
Comedian, Actor, Podcaster (*Last Week on Earth*)

Everyone wants a peak behind the curtain. You want to know what makes things tick. As a Kevin Smith fan, I can tell you that I have listened to him talk about his journey from slacker in Red Bank, New Jersey to film school dropout, to filmmaking icon. Smith himself might say he's no icon but many of us would disagree.

If you aren't a fan of Kevin Smith or at least interested in learning more about his impact upon the world of film, comics, and comedy by the time you finish this book, you might be devoid of humor.

After reading the book, I not only came away with a smile on my face, but a better and deeper affinity for him and his journey as a filmmaker and person. It makes you feel like you just sat in front of Kevin Smith and he read you the story of his life, then patted you on the head and drove away with Jason Mewes.

— James D. Creviston
Comedian, Writer, Podcaster (*The Clean Comedy Podcast*)

Cover and interior design by Jack Chappell
Cover photo © 2019 Courtesy of Andy Ford / NME
Type set in Skaters/Daddy/Avenir

ISBN: 978-0-7643-6393-1
Printed in India

Published by Schiffer Publishing, Ltd.
4880 Lower Valley Road
Atglen, PA 19310
Phone: (610) 593-1777; Fax: (610) 593-2002
Info@schifferbooks.com | www.schifferbooks.com

For our complete selection of fine books on this and related subjects, please visit our website at www.schifferbooks.com.
You may also write for a free catalog.

Schiffer Publishing's titles are available at special discounts for bulk purchases for sales promotions or premiums. Special editions, including personalized covers, corporate imprints, and excerpts, can be created in large quantities for special needs.
For more information, contact the publisher.